Edited by Corinna Downes
Typeset by Jonathan Downes
Scanning: Jessica Taylor and Emma Osborne
Cover and Internal Layout by Prudence for Gonzo MM
Using Microsoft Word 2000, Microsoft , Publisher 2000, Adobe Photoshop.

This edition published 2012 by Gonzo Multimedia

ISBN: 978-1-908728-30-2

I would like to dedicate this book to my dear wife, Norma, and my two sons, Andrew and Peter, who have made us very proud.

ABOVE: Norma, Rick and Dan in San Diego.

ABOVE: Rick looning around near Tintagel

PREFACE FROM DAN WOODING

I will never forget that day in 1968 when I walked into a shop in South Ealing, London, called The Musical Bargain Centre. I had recently joined the Middlesex County Times, a weekly newspaper that covered the London borough of Ealing, and I was on the lookout for stories. After a few months at the paper, the editor, Bert Munday, had given me South Ealing to cover, saying he hadn't had a story from this area for six months.

'See what you can get,' he told me and so, on the first day of my new 'beat', I walked along the rather non-descript South Ealing Road, visiting the various small shops there to see if I could get material, any material, to write up, but none of the owners wanted to speak to me. At each place, I was told in no uncertain terms that they 'didn't trust the press' and was shown the door. In sheer frustration, I was about to give up when I spotted a store that was selling used musical equipment and so I stepped inside and was warmly greeted by a character who called himself 'Uncle Ernie,' and who told me that he was taking care of the place on behalf the owner, Dave Simms.

'I used to pretend to play instruments during the Big Band era and that's how I earned my living,' he told me. Confused, I asked him to explain and he said, 'When a Big Band was booked, they always had to give the number of people in the band, and then when one of the musicians couldn't make it, I was recruited to pretend to play that instrument and I did that for many years. One night I would "play" the trumpet, the next the trombone, but in fact I couldn't play any instrument. But when that era ended, I was out of work, so I came here.'

As he was sharing about his most unusual make believe career, I suddenly heard the most amazing keyboard sounds coming from a back room in the shop and so I asked 'Uncle Ernie' who it was.

'Oh, that's a young kid called Ricky Wakeman,' he explained. 'He is a student at the Royal College of Music in London, and he comes in here to practice on our keyboards,' he explained. 'He is usually joined by John Entwistle, the bass player with *The Who*, who lives around the corner, but he hasn't come in today, so Ricky is here on his own.'

'Could you ask him to come out and chat with me?' I requested and soon the giant teenage figure of Ricky Wakeman appeared with a mop of blond hair and I asked him if he lived locally and he replied, 'Oh yes, I live in Northolt,' which was an area of Ealing borough.

Dan Wooding, Rick Wakeman, and Andrew Wooding in Birmingham, UK.

Having never heard anyone coax sounds out of a keyboard like he had been doing, I asked if I could interview him for the paper and his face lit up and he said, 'I've never been interviewed before.'

Soon he was telling me that he was a student at London's prestigious Royal College of Music, located close to the Royal Albert Hall, where he was studying the piano, clarinet, orchestration and modern music.

'I am paying my fees by doing sessions,' he said.

'Tell me a couple you have done recently.'

Soon he explained that he had played piano and arranged the backing for Cat Stevens' Morning Has Broken and also played Mellotron on Space Oddity for David Bowie. That was all I needed to know and a few days later, my story appeared in the paper on how local musician, young Ricky Wakeman, was watching the charts as both of these songs were shooting up to number one.

He was so thrilled with the story, that he invited me to his home and, as I sat in his front room, he played piano for me and I was absolutely mesmerised with his skill. This was a musical talent that was way beyond anything I had ever heard before and it was then our long friendship began.

I told him that I had been raised as a Christian, having been born in Nigeria of British missionary parents, and he shared that he attended the South Harrow Baptist Church, where he had been baptised and had gone on to lead the Boys' Brigade group there and was also a Sunday School teacher.

He eventually left the Royal College of Music in favour of session music work and he went on to feature on songs by artists including Ozzy Osbourne, David Bowie, *T. Rex*, and Elton John, to name just a few of his many sessions.

Not long after this he became 'Rick' rather than 'Ricky' and then in 1969 joined *The Strawbs* as the keyboard player for this folk-rock group run by Dave Cousins. He provided my wife Norma and myself with tickets for a concert at the Queen Elizabeth Hall on London's South Bank which resulted in him receiving rave reviews for his long and rather incredible solos and soon he was being trumpeted as 'Tomorrow's Next Superstar' by *Melody Maker*.

After a time with *The Strawbs*, Rick in 1971 joined the progressive rock band *Yes*, replacing their organist Tony Kaye and once again, Rick would provide tickets for their shows, and also on the first album he did with Yes called 'Fragile' he kindly gave me two mentions in the liner notes.

As his career, which also included his epic solo works like The Six Wives of Henry VIII and Journey to the Centre of the Earth, I began to realize that Rick Wakeman's talent was way beyond anyone else I had ever met and so I broached with him the possibility of writing his authorised biography, to which he agreed, and so began a labour of love which took me about five years to complete.

We then approached Elton John to see if he would write the foreword for the book – which you can read at the beginning of this biography – and Elton agreed, actually hand-wrote it and had it delivered to my office.

After the book was completed, BBC TV was doing a series called 'Success Story' produced by Alan Yentob and needed Rick to host it, but due to a few difficulties Rick was experiencing at the time, I was asked to take over and host the show, which I did. It featured me visiting all kinds of people who had worked with Rick and interviewing them for the 50-minute show. After the book came out, I moved into Fleet Street and worked for the *Sunday People*, and would regularly write stories about Rick, and when my family and I moved to Southern California back in June of 1982, Rick came to see me off on my final night in the UK.

Some years later, when I began my American non-profit organisation called ASSIST, Rick would come over and do a series of benefit concerts for us and we would be able to spend time together as we went around the States together.

Our friendship has stood the test of time and I am delighted that the book I wrote all those years ago, has now been reissued and although it only covers the earlier days of his incredible career, it gives a unique insight into the life of one of the world's greatest musicians who even today, is still wowing audiences all over the world.

The Caped Crusader is still pushing back the limits of music and is an inspiration for many of today's up-and-coming musicians, but I thought if anyone will ever reach the heights of genius that my dear friend, Rick Wakeman has.

Dan Wooding
Lake Forest, California, USA

FOREWORD

by Elton John

The first time I met Rick he played excellent organ on a track on 'The Madman Across The Water' album. My producer Gus Dudgeon had told me beforehand of this amazing keyboard player who had just joined the *Strawbs*. As I have immense respect for anyone who can play a Hammond Organ, we asked Rick to play on a session. He was, to put it mildly - annoying!

Elton John, Dan Wooding and Rick Wakeman.

Very big hands, long fingers, great technique - in fact brilliant. If people had face lifts, could I be the first person to have a hand stretch? Could I rid myself of being referred to as Old Chipolata Fingers? Quite simply, no.

Rick then went from strength to strength with the *Strawbs*, *Yes*, and more importantly, on his own. In all honesty, his 'Six Wives of Henry VIII' album is still in my top-twenty albums of all time, and I see no reason why it should not stay there for ever. I was disappointed when he didn't follow it up with 'The Ten Wives of Mickey Rooney'. Ah well, can't have everything Rick!

Rick's mastery of electronic instruments only adds to his abilities, and I think it is fair to say he was one of the reasons I stuck to the piano. I also admire his attitude to stage shows - always willing to take a gamble, but never sacrificing his musical ideals. Just as important, never losing his sense of humour and his sense of the ridiculous. Anyone who can put on an ice show at Wembley must be all right. I must add that Rick loves cars and is a fanatic when it comes to soccer. Therefore, he and I have an unbreakable bond.

It has become fashionable to knock musicians who have been around a while, and who are still determined to persevere in what they believe in. It is very easy to be misunderstood along the way, but it is vital to ignore trends and get on with what you want to do. Rick will always do this because, quite simply, he's that much better than everyone else.

ONE

The Caped Crusader

Y ou must be mad,' said Rick Wakeman's disbelieving manager Brian Lane as the blond figure wrapped his glittering shimmering cape around his giant frame and headed for the platform of London's Royal Festival Hall and his battery of electronic keyboards. And most of the London Symphony Orchestra thought they were playing for a madman - a strange caped crusader who looked like a Nordic god on a crazy ego trip. The packed audience in the London concert hall which overlooks the River Thames were just as confused, for only a lunatic would mortgage all he owned to present an idea everyone thought was crazy.

To make the evening even more bizarre, Rick Wakeman, a one-time pub pianist, had hired as the backing band for his live recording of 'Journey to the Centre of the Earth' not big name artistes like Eric Clapton and Ringo Starr, but a group which included some of his friends from the pub. Minutes before going on stage they were still playing darts in their dressing-room.

When the apprehensive applause had died down and London Symphony Orchestra conductor David Measham, a 6-foot 5-inch bearded man with the look of an Old Testament prophet, lifted his baton and launched into the show, the audience - and the orchestra - began to realize that this was no madman: they were taking part in one of the major contemporary musical events of the twentieth century. An event that was to launch Wakeman, then a relatively unknown musician, to recognition as a major rock composer, a flamboyant performer whom most progressive keyboard musicians now use as their example.

Many of the world's top orchestras were later to play his music; he was to be voted the world's top keyboard musician by the readers of leading music papers; he would capture the imagination with his flamboyant life-style which included owning a £120,000 mansion in Buckinghamshire, a £50,000 Devon farmhouse, a racehorse and twenty-one cars, including eight Rolls-Royces.

Rick Wakeman's success story, however, originated in Nantes, France, where Jules Verne was born in 1828. He was the son of a lawyer and his father expected him also to become a barrister.

Verne was addicted to sea travel and scientific study. His interests led him to create rich science fiction. In fact, many of the creations and fantasies described in his books were later actually invented. Submarines, for example, were used by Verne years before their manufacture. In the nineteenth century, Verne was

Jules Gabriel Verne
(February 8, 1828 – March 24, 1905)

writing about rockets flying around the world, television, atomic bombs, polar travel, photography, cars and travel to the centre of the world. Many of his scientific discoveries are embodied in his books, works like *20,000 Leagues Under the Sea* and *Around the World in Eighty Days*.

But it was the uncanny father of science fiction's second book - *Journey to the Centre of the Earth*, which still remains a fantasy - that captured Wakeman's imagination.

The fantastic tale described how Professor Lidinbrook and his nephew Axel discovered in Hamburg an old parchment in a twelfth-century book called *Heimskringla*, a chronicle of the Norwegian princes who ruled Iceland.

This parchment, decoded into Latin and translated by Axel, proved to be written by a sixteenth-century alchemist and read:

'Descend into the crater of Sneffels Yokul, over which the shadow of Scatuaris falls before the Kalends of July, bold traveller, and you will reach the centre of the earth. I have done this - Arne Saknussemm.'

(Sneffels is a 5,000- foot-high mountain in Iceland, an extinct volcano which last erupted in 1229.)

And so Wakeman decided to pay his musical tribute to the epic journey from Hamburg to Iceland and then down to the world's core.   It was one of the first complete concept albums in the history of rock music to capture the imagination.

'I got personal confirmation that I should go ahead with 'Journey' after visiting pubs and talking to people about my idea,' said Wakeman, his face twitching nervously as he recalled the risks he took putting on this giant production. 'I asked if they had heard of Jules Verne, and everyone said they had. So I asked if they had heard of the book *Journey to the Centre of the Earth* and again most people had heard of it. But hardly anyone knew what the story was about, so I felt that served my purposes well, for I believed that for a concept album you needed a title everyone had heard of but basically they 'didn't know much about.'

So Wakeman read and re-read Verne's book and then began making a summary of it. He whittled the story down until it finally became the narration read by top film actor David Hemmings[*] on the album.

---

[*] David Hemmings (1941 – 2003) was an English film, theatre and television actor as well as a film and television director and producer. He is noted for his role as the photographer in the drama mystery-thriller film *Blowup* (1966), directed by Michelangelo Antonioni. Early in his career, Hemmings was a boy soprano appearing in operatic roles. In his later acting career, he was known for his distinctive eyebrows and gravelly voice.

'I then began to hear the sounds of the music in my brain. They were beautiful sounds that kept floating around my head - but they were sounds I realized could never be reproduced just by a rock band. They included orchestral sounds. So I decided I needed an orchestra and being a lover of top orchestras and not the sort of guy who could really work with the East Hackney Sinfonia - although if they existed they would have probably been cheaper - I thought of the London Symphony Orchestra, and David Measham.'[*]

The London Symphony Orchestra is the city's oldest. It was formed in 1904 and has become one of the world's most famous orchestras with more than twenty-nine overseas tours to its credit. But how could Wakeman persuade an organization of that calibre to play his music? Who could help him make the approach?

'I was convinced David Measham would be the key,' said Wakeman. 'Although he is a classical musician and conductor, I knew he was also heavily involved and genuinely interested in the contemporary music scene. I had played for him on the Christmas 'Tommy' show at the Rainbow Theatre, London, and so knew him a little. I phoned him and asked him to come and see me.' (The original contact was made through Lou Reizner[**] who was responsible for the orchestral productions of 'Tommy'.)

In the meantime Wakeman busied himself writing down 'Journey' 'mind sounds', as he calls them, in a music book.

'I sat at the piano and frantically scribbled down the notes as fast as they appeared in my brain,' he said. Then he made a rough demo tape using a Revox tape recorder of the short score on Moog, Mellotron, Fender Rhodes and Clavinette.

'David finally came round to my house but warned me he had a very busy schedule and might not be able to get involved,' said Wakeman. 'He sat there in dead silence as I played him this rough old tape

---

*. David Michael Lucian Measham (1937 – 2005) was a British-Australian conductor and violinist.

Measham was born in Nottingham, England, to a musical family. His father had trained as an opera singer and his mother was a pianist. He began violin studies at age 7, and first conducted at age 13. He attended the Guildhall School of Music and Drama, London, where he studied with Norman Del Mar. He then became a section violinist with the BBC Symphony Orchestra. He served with the City of Birmingham Symphony Orchestra as co-leader (1963–1967) alongside John Georgiadis. He became principal second violin with the London Symphony Orchestra (LSO) in 1967 following Neville Marriner's departure. Measham worked as a conductor with non-classical artists such as the saxophonist Ornette Coleman (The Skies Of America, 1972), Pete Townshend (Tommy, 1972), Neil Young (Harvest, 1972) and on a full orchestral version of *The Beatles'* Sgt. Pepper's Lonely Hearts Club Band. In 1974, Measham conducted the LSO on Rick Wakeman's Journey to the Centre of the Earth, touring America and Japan and later the New World Symphony Orchestra on The Myths and Legends of King Arthur and the Knights of the Round Table.

Measham died of cancer of the pancreas, in Perth. His early marriage to the soprano Susan Shoemaker ended in divorce. His two children from his marriage, Aaron and Guenevere, survive him.

**. Lou Reizner (1934 - 1977) was a record producer, A&R executive and head of Mercury Records European operations. As a producer, he is perhaps best known for Rod Stewart's first two solo albums, for the orchestral version of *The Who's* rock opera Tommy, and Rick Wakeman's 'Journey to the Centre of the Earth'. As an A&R executive, he signed *Van der Graaf Generator*, and *Smile* (the precursor to *Queen*, and arranged a US deal for David Bowie. He even co-wrote, sang on and produced two tracks for the film 'The Italian Job' (another Quincy Jones film), which were issued as a single in 1969. He had one child, Claudia Collingbourne.

He also worked on the soundtrack to 'All This and World War II' a 1976 film comprising 20th Century Fox World War II newsreels, set to *Beatles* songs, re-recorded by current artists such as *The Bee Gees*, Rod Stewart, *Status Quo* and Peter Gabriel.

and explained where the different orchestral parts came in. When it finished, he looked at me and said, "Rick, that *will* work. It will take a lot of work and I'd love to do it with you." I was really knocked out. It was at that moment that I knew which direction my career was going to go.'

But there were still many more problems before a concert could be put on. The committee of the London Symphony Orchestra had to be convinced that they could get involved and Wakeman's manager Brian Lane and his record company, A&M, had to be convinced that this was a project that would work.

Wakeman smiles as he remembers the first time he broached the subject of 'Journey' with 'deal-a-day' Lane, now rated among the top five rock managers in the world.

'I was in his office and he asked me if I had any ideas for a new album to follow 'Six Wives of Henry VIII',' said Rick. 'I said, "It's going to be 'Journey to the Centre of the Earth', the Jules Verne classic." He said, "Great, when are you going into the studio to do it?" I told him that it wasn't going to be done in a studio, but live. So Brian got into his usual pose when we talk – head in hands – and ordered a large brandy from his secretary.

I continued, "I'd like you to book the Royal Festival Hall, the London Symphony Orchestra, the full English Chamber Choir and David Measham."'

Wakeman added that he wanted Irish actor Richard Harris to narrate the concert. 'When I left his office they were still trying to bring Brian round.'

Rick realized he needed help with the scoring of the music, so he contacted an arranger with whom he had worked on recording sessions - Wil Malone, who had been responsible for most of the orchestration on 'Tommy'.

'Wil came to my Devon farmhouse and we talked the project over. I asked him if he could do it and he told me it needed at least three months' work. "When do you want it by?" he said. "Next Friday," I replied. But when he heard my fee he agreed to try!'

Malone linked with another arranger, Danny Beckerman, and they worked night and day to complete the orchestral score in record time, a feat Rick will always remember with deep appreciation.

But Wakeman still had to pick the musicians for his small rock ensemble. Having played on 'Tommy' and on numerous sessions with some of the world's top rock stars, he knew he could have had the pick of them. But never one to conform, he picked a bunch of unknowns with whom he had jammed at a country pub in Buckinghamshire called the *Valiant Trooper*.

'I'd played with them for fun quite a bit on Sunday evenings,' said Wakeman. 'We used to jam in the bar and people would come from miles around to hear us. We then held a collection to buy a special mobile chair for an invalid. We got so popular that people would spill out on to the car park. It was almost impossible to get near the bar. One Sunday evening I was playing keyboards with the lads when I thought, "They could play 'Journey' for me. I'm sure they could do the concert and do it well."'

Afterwards, Wakeman rounded up the group, Ashley Holt, Roger Newell and Barney James, and asked them if they'd like to do 'a little gig with me'. Of course they would.

'Where is it to be?' asked Roger Newell, the bass guitarist, innocently.

'The Royal Festival Hall with the London Symphony Orchestra,' replied Wakeman. The shocked band retired for further drinks.

Wakeman then assembled them for a rehearsal and found they were just right for his band. He added top session guitarist Mike Egan, and Gary Pickford Hopkins from a group called *Wild Turkey* as another vocalist to combine with Ashley Holt. Now he had to break the news of his unknown band to manager Lane.

'After Brian had recovered from my previous visit, he agreed to talk again about the "Journey" project,' said Rick. 'He told me that there would be loads of big names who would like to do the concert, but I told him I didn't want them. I didn't think it would work with "faces". He sat there stunned as I went through each member of my group, and then he said, "Where did you find them?" I said, "At a little pub called the *Valiant Trooper,* Holmer Green." He said, "What are you going to call them? *Time Gentleman Please?*"

'Brian took a deep breath and added, "Do you realize Rick that you are going on at the Royal Festival Hall with the London Symphony Orchestra and David Measham to do a live album which we all hope will sell around the world – and you've chosen yourself a band like that?" I asked him to bear with me and he'd see that they could do the job. I knew deep down they could, even though most of them had never seen a symphony orchestra before, let alone played with one.'

As the group rehearsed incessantly, Lane found that Richard Harris unfortunately wasn't available to narrate the concert, so David Hemmings was approached and readily agreed to do it. Ironically he had exactly the voice that Rick had envisaged for the work, and David Hemmings's enthusiasm went a long way to making the extravaganza work.

Derek Green, British head of A&M Records was naturally put in the picture about 'Journey'. Rick visited him at his New King's Road, London, office, to sell him the idea. Green, after listening patiently, turned to him and said, 'O.K. Rick, you are going to perform a live album, a new piece which you've written. And you're going to do it with a symphony orchestra? Do you realize the cost of that? Plus a sixty-eight-piece choir?'

Like Lane, Green was convinced big names were crucial to the success of such a risky project. He told me: 'I asked Rick why he didn't use the guys from *Yes*, who he was now playing with, and he said he didn't want them because people would say the music and the production was either a *Yes* project, or because he was using the group's strength to put himself across musically. So I suggested people like Ringo Starr and Eric Clapton. I knew they'd love to play, but he said, "No, I've got some mates from the pub to do it."' That was the way he described it to me and I couldn't believe it. I immediately phoned Brian Lane and said: "Do you know what Rick's planning to do?" As we discussed it we were both really wiped out. I said, "Brian, do you know these guys? They've never performed a concert before. They're unheard of."

'I knew we were about to record what could be one of the great events in contemporary music and Rick was going to take a chance with unknown musicians. It was too frightening to contemplate.'

However, A&M , in trepidation, agreed to record the concert for a live album and Ronnie Lane's mobile recording unit was booked.

'Money was a big problem because the whole project was costing about £40,000,' said Rick, 'I had to sell some of my cars and mortgage myself up to the hilt to help finance the whole thing.' Rick decided that the performance would be greatly enhanced by clips of the Hollywood film of *Journey to the Centre of the Earth* being flashed on to a screen behind the Festival Hall stage. 'Some of the band came with me to see the film at a little preview theatre in Soho,' said Wakeman. 'We had to stop the film about ten times because we were rolling about on the floor. We couldn't work out how you could be in the middle of the earth, like Pat Boone was, and still have a Brylcreem bounce on your hair. The film was made at a time when it was the thing to have a major star like James Mason in the film and also a pop star.'

Wakeman didn't like the film one little bit. 'I had really got into the book and I knew the story inside out and backwards, so when I saw the film I was disgusted. They had unnecessarily altered the story and had even started it at Edinburgh University instead of at Hamburg. It was an abortion of the book.' Rick picked a few clips from the film to illustrate his music - and vowed never to see the film again.

The worry of the extravagant project was now beginning to take its toll on Wakeman's health. A few days before the concert, rock journalist Tony Tyler was shocked to see how ill Wakeman had become. Tyler dropped into one of the full rehearsals with the orchestra and choir and said, 'I've never seen him look worse than when we met during the rehearsal. The famous hair resembled a can of yellow paint poured over his skull, the once-ruddy complexion was a delicate shade of avocado and that fine Guardsman figure had degenerated into a giant, shambling question-mark. He has an ulcer, he told me. Certainly his physical degeneration had plenty to do with his work output. No shiftless poseur he.'

During rehearsal, Wakeman worked round the clock constantly picking upon every tiny blunder by his other musicians, trying it again from the top with almost manic calm and a constant flow of canned beer. Six exhausting dress rehearsals took place before the show was ready to go on.

Tyler went on: 'I watched him rehearse himself and his band into a coma; I watched him run through the "Centre of the Earth" score in company with the London Symphony Orchestra at a dress rehearsal till even the veteran cellists of that worthy orchestra were shuffling their bows and glancing at the clock. At no time did he blow it - not once - but some of us had real fears for his health. Whether it would stand up to the strain.'

Wakeman was in for a big blow on the day of the concert. 'The orchestra had to do two concerts on the same night for me and the idea was to record both of them and then use the best show, but the union guy told me that if both houses were recorded the orchestra wanted double pay. I was absolutely shattered. With the expenses already phenomenal I had to take the frightening decision of only recording the second performance and hoping there weren't too many mistakes. It was a real shock to me and I've never forgiven those responsible for doing that to me. I don't think I ever will.'

Although he did not know it at the time, Rick's health was soon to crack up completely and exhaustion was taking a heavy toll on him. Another more immediate problem was his teeth. Rick has always had a phobia about going to the dentist. 'My teeth were like a broken-down graveyard and I was in terrible pain. I had three abscesses at once and they had to give me five injections to get me on stage,' said Rick. Even before the concert started, the overwrought Wakeman was mentally and physically shattered.

He said: 'I have never, ever, been so scared as I was about that concert, I had played concerts before nearly 100,000 people in the States, but never had I been so terrified. The whole thing had developed into a nightmare, literally. I didn't sleep at all for three nights before the gig. In fact all the arrangements for the concert were messed up. The tickets went on sale while I was on tour with *Yes*, and when I got back I found that I couldn't even get seats for my Mum and Dad. In the end I had to buy some tickets for £15 each from a ticket tout.'

Rick arrived at the Royal Festival Hall at 8am on that life-changing day. A leaden sky loomed over

London as he began to get himself mentally attuned to this make-or-break effort. Rehearsals began early and went on throughout the day.

After the final run-through a tired Wakeman told Roy Hill, of *Record Mirror*: 'It's just right now, it should hopefully hit the right peak tonight.'

The two performances on that freezing Friday night on 18 January 1974, were at 6pm and 8pm. Last-minute checks were made on his battery of keyboards – a Hammond Organ, Fender, RMI and Hohner electric pianos, three Mellotrons, two Mini Moogs, a honky-tonk piano and two grands.

The first part of the show was mainly Wakeman playing excerpts from his hit album 'Six Wives of Henry VIII' and a couple of humorous vignettes. Then for the second half the orchestra tuned up and the choir assembled. The band took up their place and by the time that Measham walked on, followed by the man in the cape, with so much at stake, there were more than 150 on stage. The second part was what the 3,000 sell-out first house were after, the world premiere of 'Journey'. There was actor David Hemmings on smooth, Valentine Dyall*-style narration, and the cast of Cecil B. De Mille proportion supporting Wakeman's musical potholing. The audience showed their appreciation of the piece at the end of the first house with great gusts of applause, ranging from Peter Sellers's polite sturdy clapping to the dedicated Wakemanites yelling of 'Brilliant, brilliant'.

But now it was the second performance that was to be vital to Wakeman. For if he blew this one, the album was off.

Tyler attended the show and wrote in the *New Musical Express*:

> They wheeled out the orchestra and choir. David Hemmings took his place in the Peacock Throne with the narrative script settled comfortably on his lap in best fire-side manner. On came Wakeman and group again and the conductor lifted his baton and ....

* Valentine Dyall (7 May 1908 – 24 June 1985) was an English character actor, the son of veteran actor Franklin Dyall. Dyall was especially popular as a voice actor, due to his very distinctive sepulchral voice, he was known for many years as "The Man in Black", narrator of the BBC Radio horror series *Appointment With Fear*.

This ambitious piece of music is another proposition entirely from 'Six Wives'. For a start, it's orchestrated for soloist, soloist-with-trio, trio, choir, vocalists, orchestra and narrator - all controlled by the conductor (who takes cues in his turn from the narrator and from Wakeman) and by Wakeman himself (who takes cues from the conductor and from the film screen).

This screen was used to display fragments from the film spectacular of the same name and the whole parcel, amazingly stayed together with only a single mistaken chirp from the guitar and another from the drums during its entire life.

Musically, it's strong on melody and organization. The French horns introduce a two-bar theme at the very beginning, this is picked up by the orchestra, finally by the soloist and is modified, inverted and finally resolved in grandeur at the end of the work.

Wakeman, very properly, confines his soloing to occasional tailed sprints, reserving the great part of his arsenal of ivories for plenty of fluent *obbligato* work over the orchestra and the two solo vocalists. Passages end, chords are sustained - and these gaps are used by Hemmings for narration (the narrative precised by Wakeman from Verne's original) the pause is held . . . and in comes the orchestra again.

The experiment worked very well. There were no embarrassing excesses and what could have been a cumbersome mishmash turned out to display heels of quicksilver. In fact, I was just getting into it when it ended with a Wagnerian series of chords and cymbal crashes.

And as the echo of the cymbal died away the audience broke into wild applause and rose to its feet. The applause lasted for several minutes and brought Wakeman back for a planned encore which he called 'The Pearl And Dean Unfinished Piano Concerto in C Major' - a short and intensely funny piece for a piano-with-orchestra which kicked off with the theme from Opal Fruits ('Made to Make Your Mouth Water') took in Fairy Liquid ('Hands That Do Dishes Can Feel As Soft As Your Face') and finished finally, with the cymbal player doing the last-minute crunch from the Murray Mints ad. ('They're Too Good To Hurry').

There was again uproar as Wakeman stumbled off stage in triumph. And as if by command, the orchestra stood up and gave this blond whirling Dervish the kind of standing ovation they usually reserve for superstars like Menuhin and Previn.

Rodney Gilchrist wrote in the *Daily Mail*: 'For the young blond-haired Nordic-looking figure in the shimmering cape standing in the spotlight at the Royal Festival Hall it was the realization of a Walter Mitty-style fantasy.'

Rick remembered nothing about it. A party had been laid on for him afterwards, but the semi-conscious Wakeman had to be driven back to his Buckinghamshire home by Ros, his anxious wife, as the party guests waited in vain for his appearance.

Several days later Wakeman recovered enough to hear the tape of the concert. The tape was then to be tightly and expertly mixed by Wakeman and Paul Tregurtha.

'Everyone was deliriously happy with the concert', said Rick, 'but then we heard all the mistakes. There weren't a lot, ironically, but there were enough. I refused point-blank to re-record any of the concert. I said, "It's a live album and it stays a live album." And that mix was the hardest I've ever had to do in my life, but it was worth it when it was all done.

'Other technical difficulties were that all the gear was hired apart from mine. It was meant to be a one-off and the band's equipment was not suitable for the Royal Festival Hall, though it went down a treat at the Valiant Trooper. So everything was hired - we'd never played a gig in a large place together - in fact the biggest that the lads had ever done on their own was in a village hall in front of a couple of hundred people. Theoretically, all the odds were against us.

'The main problem was that we had to do the vocals again because somebody kicked out the vocals leads, so we only had half the vocals. So we had to match up one half of the vocals with the other. I didn't like doing it, but we had no choice. And a snare drum had broken half-way through 'The Battle', so off the main master on to another master machine we recorded the drum track and made a sort of jigsaw cut of the tape, cut out the actual drum track from the middle of the tape, stuck in the drum track that we'd re-recorded off another machine - about an eighth of an inch for 50 feet. We even cut out single notes and stuck them in. It was horrific - it was absolutely unbelievable. Paul hardly spoke a word throughout the whole exercise. He'd say, "We can't mix this, there's no drums there", and I'd say, "Let's just check the tempo of the next bit." If the tempo was the same we'd record that drum track on to another machine, take the snare drum out and slot a new one in. He'd look at me, and we knew one another very well by then. He knew I wasn't joking. So he shook his head, ordered a large vodka, and about nine hours later, we'd done it. And then we'd move on and find a similar problem on the next bit. When we finished mixing that album it was pure relief.'

When the album was released, Wakeman and A&M waited to see what would happen. The music critics, on the whole, gave it a good reception. Derek Jewell in the *Sunday Times* wrote:

> 'I missed the event . . . on record it comes over magnificently. Wakeman the conservatoire-trained keyboard virtuoso of Yes, has written a striking work which only occasionally lapses into pretentiousness. In particular he blends the sounds of his electronic keyboards with the sharp brass and urgent strings of the London Symphony Orchestra.'

Chris Welch, in *Melody Maker*, said:

> 'As far as popular music is concerned, Rick's composition for choir, orchestra and group is entertaining, fresh, and disarmingly unpretentious. There are no attempts to be arty, clever, or super-technical. This could be a score for a Hollywood musical - tuneful, but with epic overtones. There's no doubt Rick was inspired by Jules Verne's delightful tale, so long a firm childhood and adult favourite, with a broad score for musical picture painting.

> His imagination has been given free rein with such episodes as the descent into an extinct volcano in search of a route to the earth's centre, the party losing their way, finding a subterranean ocean, witnessing a battle of sea monsters and being finally ejected back to the surface by an eruption.

> The very familiarity of the story, and Rick's close observance of its detail, engenders a warmth to the work, which made it such a resounding success as a concert performance.

A phone call at Rick's farmhouse in Devon shattered his peace. He was almost over the strain of recent events, when Terry O'Neil from A&M's London office told Rick: 'I just thought I'd tell you that 'Journey' has just hit number-one in the British album charts.'

Rick sank into the chair near to tears. It had all been worthwhile and the album just kept selling and selling, something like two million worldwide at the last count. It was nominated for the American Music Industry's coveted 'Grammy' award for 1974, won an Ivor Novello award in Britain, topped music polls, as well as bringing in Gold Discs from around the world. It had been a worthwhile 'Journey'. Commented Rick: 'The whole thing was like a fairytale. A fairytale that came true. .. .'

TWO

Take off with the Concords

Post-war life was hectic for Cyril and Mildred Wakeman, Rick's parents. They had just left their first home, a cramped London flat, for a tidy new semi-detached house in Northolt, Middlesex, a fast-growing suburb on the western outskirts of London for young marrieds wanting to swop the smoke and grime of the city in the late 1940s for the relative luxury of fresh air and room to breathe.

Cyril, a stocky man with a full and friendly face and an ample figure, was then a builder's clerk with a company in London's scruffy East End. He wanted to build a new life for his wife and his eagerly awaited child, and they settled down to await the birth of their first-born. Rick was born on 18th May 1949, at Perivale Maternity Hospital, and the doctors surprised the family by explaining why the boy would not stop crying.

'He's got an over-active brain,' said the doctor. Rick began talking very early, but it was more than a year before he started crawling, and then it was . . . backwards.

"We always knew where he was because he would crawl backwards under something, get stuck and start crying,' said Mrs Mildred Wakeman. 'He never had the sense to turn round and come out. He would cry until someone came to help him.' It did not endear the infant to an already harried father.

Like most men in Britain at the time, Cyril Wakeman had served the war period in the services - the Army to be precise. Cyril played the piano in his regimental dance band and, back in Civvy Street, he'd used a £100 'thank you' to buy a prestigious Bechstein upright piano.

As Rick approached his seventh birthday Cyril was keen for him to learn, although his local piano teacher, Mrs Dorothy Symes, had a long list of potential Rubinsteins all waiting to be taught their scales and *arpeggios*.

But Rick soon got his chance and began his weekly hour-long lessons at Mrs Symes's large house in Harrow, a brisk four-minute walk from the Wakeman semi. Mrs Symes, who taught under her maiden name of Dorothy Copleston, introduced the beanstalk blond to the joys, and otherwise, of classical music in a special music room built on to her home. The room, about the size of a double bedroom, contained two upright Bluthners and a Bechstein upright.

One of Richard's fellow pupils

'During the thirteen years I had Richard (all his early friends still call him Richard) for music lessons he received a strict classical training and passed all the Associated Board of Royal Schools of Music exams from Grade I to Grade VIII in both theory and practical,' recalled Mrs Symes. 'In fact he passed everything with a distinction.'

Mrs Symes remembers the tousled-haired Rick as an 'enjoyable pupil to teach, full of fun and with a good sense of humour'. But she had one criticism of him, and that was his lack of self-discipline in practice. 'He hated practising his scales and *arpeggios* and his exam marks were always lower for scales, than anything else,' said Mrs Symes.

The trouble was, said Mrs Symes, that Rick was always changing things and playing them the way he wanted to, which revealed his gift for composition. 'His active musical mind was always exploring new musical avenues through these arrangements and compositions,' she said. 'But they were not for my ear, I never heard them. People who passed Richard's house often told me they'd heard through the window a remarkable adaptation of a classical piece. I usually said, "It's nothing that I taught him."'

Besides his scales, the gangling Wakeman had another problem. 'He had great difficulty getting his long legs under the keyboard,' said Mrs Symes. 'That meant he had to sit quite a way back from the piano. Fortunately he had long arms.'

After about three years, Rick got his first taste of playing before an audience. Mrs Symes entered her precocious pupil, in the Southall Music Festival, one of the many festivals where eager mums went through agony as fame beckoned to their offspring. Rick won. It was to be the first in a long string of successes on the highly competitive circuit.

Rick recalls those triumphant days: 'The festivals used to be in dismal halls, in front of about half a dozen people, usually pushy mums. The same young hopefuls went to all the festivals, and it was a bit like looking down the form card on the racing page. You thought: "He's the 7-4 favourite, she's 10-1. They're in with a good chance." I wasn't nervous - I used to love it. I like playing in front of people. It sounds incredibly egotistical, but I think when you're a kid you are. And Mrs Symes was like another mother to me. I played for her as well as myself. I think she enjoyed success as well and there was always a somewhat less-than-friendly rivalry between the local music teachers.

'You had to play a set piece according to your class and within three years I had won thirty on the trot. I came to think that I would win every time. Well, I went along for one and came second, and that really brought me down. That day I knew how Avis felt about Hertz. But Mrs Symes said: "You're going in for these festivals to get constructive criticism from the judges, that's all." From that day on I looked at the festivals in a different light.'

Mrs Symes recalled Rick's prowess at the contests in South and West London, as well as outlying areas

like Watford and Uxbridge. She said that the festivals gave him the 'nerve and composure' vital for someone playing to a critical audience and they taught him to accept criticism as well as praise from mainly top musicians. Mrs Symes gave him a vital insight into classics and taught him the technique necessary to interpret and play the music of Bach, Scarlatti, Handel, Haydn, Mozart, Beethoven, as well as the romantic and modern composers.

Rick's musical ability was quickly spotted by the minister of the local church he attended as a teenager – South Harrow Baptist. The Rev. Frank Taylor, then minister and now chaplain of a Harrow college, told me: 'He would often play at the youth club. His music had a kind of abandon about it. He was completely lost when he was on the piano.

'I suppose that is the way he communicated best in those days. He just used to sit down there and his fingers would fly and he would be lost to the world. He played fantastically and the others would gather round him and listen to his music.'

His Boys Brigade* leader from those days, Mr Hugh Blanch, said music was not Rick's only talent. 'Apart from his musical talent, which seems to have been born in him, I think his other natural calling was as a leader,' said Mr Blanch.

'At annual camps his leadership ability always shone through. At camp though, I discovered one of his weaknesses - he hates getting up in the morning!

I recall occasions when the bugler had to actually stand in his tent and play Reveille in order to wake him up. Needless to say when it was time for lights out he didn't want to go to sleep.

'At night he also seemed to suffer from the cold. I think he used to wear twice as many clothes to go to bed as he did in the daytime.' (This, recalls Rick, was so that he did not have to wake up the other boys in the tent when he got dressed to sneak out for a quick drink at the *Anchor* pub in the aptly named village of Beer, Devon, after lights out.)

'Rick took the religious side of the Boys Brigade fairly seriously,' said Mr Blanch. 'I always imagined this was as a sense of duty but later I found, with great pleasure, that there was much more to it and that he wanted to be baptised. I think this made quite a difference to him.'

* The Boys' Brigade (BB) is an interdenominational Christian youth organisation, conceived by William Alexander Smith to combine drill and fun activities with Christian values. Following its inception in Glasgow in 1883, the BB quickly spread across the United Kingdom and became a worldwide organisation by the early 1890s. As of 2003, there were 500,000 Boys' Brigade members in 60 countries.

In fact, before making his career as a full-time rock star, Rick insisted on being baptised by immersion at his church. He seemed to sense that he would soon be so involved in the pop world that he wanted protection - a kind of religious insurance policy.

He donned a white robe one Sunday night when he was eighteen years old and took the plunge in front of a packed church.

Rock music became more and more of an attraction to Rick. It once even resulted in him prancing around a local hall at the age of fourteen, wearing a gas mask.

He had joined a five-piece group called the *Atlantic Blues*, and they rehearsed in the dingy Civil Defence hall across the road from Rick's house.

The musical prowess of the five-piece band soon came to the notice of a London organization, which hired them for a twelve-month residency.

'It wasn't exactly the "Talk of the Town" said Wakeman. 'In fact it was at the Neasden Club for the Mentally Handicapped.'

But those twelve months as pianist and singer at Neasden began to teach young Wakeman about the discipline of working within a group. And although the Neasden gig each week was enjoyable, his big dream was to play in front of his friends in one of the local Northolt pubs ... and one day that dream came true.

'We were booked as the interval band at the Byron, which meant we filled in during the break for the main band,' said Rick. 'The room was full when we arrived. And we soon discovered to our horror that the stage was already packed with the other group's equipment. So we had to set up at the other end of the room. To make things worse, there was no spare piano. So the band played at the end of the room and I played from the stage.

It was most probably the world's first real-life stereo gig. It didn't last long. Soon after I started singing 'High Heel Sneakers' a tremendous fight broke out on the floor and the police were called, and about half the audience were arrested. We just packed up and went home. It was a very disappointing local debut for me.'

Wakeman formed his first big band at the age of fifteen. It was hastily formed after Rick was told there would be a £40 fee for the band signed up to play for the annual Drayton Manor Grammar School dance in Hanwell, West London.

'I know a very good group who would give you a great evening's entertainment,' Rick told the teacher organizer. 'It's my band – *Curdled Milk*.'

What Rick did not tell the organizer was the *Curdled Milk* - jokingly named after *Cream*, then Britain's top rock band - did not actually exist.

The organiser accepted Rick's offer, and soon Wakeman collected together an assortment of competent musicians around him, including members of a Salvation Army rock band who also entertained at the Neasden Mentally Handicapped Club.

So with *Curdled Milk* formed and rehearsed, Rick borrowed the family Standard Ensign car so he could arrive in the style befitting a rock star.

Unfortunately, he parked it in the middle of the headmaster's flower bed. When an irate teacher stopped the music and called for the culprit to own up, Rick tried to.

'Who did it?' yelled the teacher.

Rick sitting at his keyboard, tried to attract the red-faced teacher's attention, but was told to be quiet. Again he tried. Finally he shouted: 'It's my bloody car.' Much of the band's hard-earned money that night went to pay for new rose bushes.

Shortly after, Wakeman was offered the chance of earning £5 a week playing with *The Concords*, a

slightly more polished outfit, playing a mixture of dance and pop music for local functions. He decided to play for both groups. (*The Concords* later changed to the *Concord Quartet* because they discovered there was another group with the same name.)

Rick finally left the *Atlantic Blues* and played full-time with the *Concord Quartet*, which later had another Wakeman in its line-up - Rick's cousin Alan, who played saxophone and clarinet, and is now a top saxophonist.

Money from a twice-weekly booking at the Brent Social Club, Wembley, enabled him to buy his first electronic instrument - a £40 Hohner Pianet (an electric piano).

So in his early teens. Rick was already making quite a name for himself in the rock field, as well as with his classical performances. (He won 100 certificates at the music festivals, as well as twenty medals and cups.) But he found another field, the sports field, that also began to draw him like a magnet.

'If he was practising the piano and somebody knocked on the door with a football under their arm he was gone. He would come back and do it later, but sport had precedence.'

At thirteen or fourteen Rick first noticed the attractions of the opposite sex. And most of his friends were giving up piano lessons to concentrate on more interesting pastimes. One girlfriend called Jane Augustin from South Harrow was responsible for giving the future rock star a new name. She began calling him Ricky instead of Richard, and soon it was latched on to by everyone.

Mrs Wakeman recalls those teenage days. 'One day Mrs Symes phoned me up and said I was wasting my money and her time because Richard wasn't practising,' she said.

We said to him: "If you're not interested in music, what are you going to do?" We could never get him to discuss anything.'

And Rick admits what a problem he was: 'I was a horror at grammar school. I worked hard in the first year, then eased up. It was almost too late afterwards. I knew they wouldn't throw me out, because they wanted me to go to the Royal College of Music. So I took terrible advantage of the teachers.'

Mrs Wakeman remembers: 'I asked Richard: "Have you decided to do music then?" and he said: "It's all I can do."

'First he had to get his "A" levels which meant passing eight music exam grades. He'd finished six and didn't bother to do the seventh. His school music teacher told me: "He's done nothing much for a couple of years now. Just muddled through." It meant he had to do two year's work in ten months.'

So they went back to Mrs Symes for extra lessons, and she pointed out the size of the task. 'I will do all I can for Richard. but it will be difficult. If I ring you up and say he's not working hard enough you must accept my word for it,' Mrs Symes told Mrs Wakeman.

It looked impossible, but he got the spur he needed from his school music teacher, Mr Herrera. It came in the form of a bet, and Rick, always one for a gamble, responded.

'Mr Herrera bet ten shillings [50p], a fortune then, that I wouldn't pass my music "A" level,' said Rick. 'I went home and looked at the syllabus. I thought: "There's no way I'll pass." But I worked hard at home, though I still didn't go to his lessons - I hadn't been for ages.'

The bet did the trick and after he'd passed, Mr Herrera sent him the money and a note which said: 'I never thought you'd do it, but this was the only way.'

Another reason for this about-turn was the threat by his father that, instead of having a successful musical career, he would have to get a job with his building firm.

Rick said; 'Over my dead body.'

So his mind was made up. He was going to the Royal College of Music. He was going to be a concert pianist.

THREE

Out of Tune at the Royal College

Rick had one more hurdle to cross before he got his coveted college place – an interview in front of a panel of learned professors.

Although Rick was certain his piano would impress the examiners, he was delighted when they let him off the other test - on the clarinet.

At his Royal College of Music interview, Rick knew the clarinet was very much his second instrument. All the students had to study two instruments, and prove their competence to the examining board.

'I had a stinking cold and it was their idea for me not to play the clarinet,' Wakeman recalls. 'I had taken it along with me and I was quite willing to play. I said, "I play second clarinet in the school orchestra very badly, and mime most of the time," which was more or less true – but they roared with laughter, gave me a very high grade on the clarinet and said they were sure I was very good at it and was just being incredibly modest.'

Rick enrolled in this famous seat of musical learning, close to the Royal Albert Hall, London, on a performance course, but almost immediately decided to switch to the teacher's course. For within hours of joining, he had experienced the old fears of his school days that he might not make the grade as a concert pianist.

'Very soon I was convinced, with all this talent around, that I wouldn't. I also desperately wanted security, and knew being a music teacher was a much safer job.'

Rick went on; "The Royal College of Music was a cross between some of the best days I ever had and some of the worst. I went through every emotion. The first few weeks I cried with excitement. This was followed by disillusionment, periods of feeling very unhappy, then very happy - everything. The first few months was like a jigsaw puzzle coming together, the music history I learnt, the "A" levels, the festivals.

But the disillusionment was that out of the 250 college newcomers, whittled down from thousands, I found fifty were as good as you, 100 weren't so good and the other 100 were a hell of a lot better.'

Rick described the course as 'walking disaster'. 'They treated you like a child,' he said. "Everybody has their pride – and nobody wants to be treated like a child, although, to be fair, I very often deserved the treatment I got.'

One hangover from his rebellious days at school was his famous, long, golden locks. A college professor complained about the length of his hair, which did not even reach his shoulders in those days. Rick had intended to have it cut that very day, but was so annoyed at being told what to do that he left it to grow to almost waist level. It stayed that way for eight years.

He tried to get rock and jazz clubs going at the college, but failed. Ironically, when he went back to the Royal College of Music a few years later, everyone seemed to have long hair and pop music was flourishing. A professor rubbed it in by saying - 'You were here at the wrong time, weren't you, Wakeman?'

Because of his frustration at the college, he developed a couldn't-care-less attitude, and spent a lot of time in nearby bars. One day he got drunk before a clarinet lesson, and his befuddled mind had great trouble in working out how to put the instrument together. He played three notes, and then passed out. But despite this, his clarinet professor, Basil Tchaikov, remembers him with some affection.

'Rick worked very consistently, but it gradually became apparent he was more interested in pop,' he said. 'And it came as something of a surprise to see that rather exotic image which he now projects, the sort of picture you get on his record sleeves.'

The professor was right about his pop leanings, for Wakeman, the college drop-out, began to spend much of his spare time in an eccentric music shop in South Ealing, London, called the Musical Bargain Centre. It was run by musician David Simms, aided and abetted by 'Uncle' Ernie - the only name he ever uses. Ernie, a bearded Geordie[*], couldn't play a note, but his claim to fame in the business was that he knew many top musicians and made great coffee.

'Rick used to enjoy messing around on our various instruments, and if I wanted a guitar tuned, he'd do it for me. I was impressed by his versatility,' said Ernie.

'One day he picked up a banjo and we went outside busking. I held the hat as he played. An old lady came waltzing down from the greengrocer's and stopped right in front of Rick. She opened her purse and said, "I can't afford very much on my pension, but there you are dear." And she dropped a threepenny bit in the hat! Rick immediately stopped playing, picked up the money and went indoors. He didn't even give me a penny for my troubles.'

While still at the Royal College, Dave Simms gave Rick an evening job with his dance band. 'I was short a piano player and I asked him to sit in,' said Dave. 'He turned up for the audition all pimply faced, wearing drainpipe trousers, winklepicker shoes, and called me "Mr Simms". But his natural talent became obvious from the start, in fact it was just astronomical. The band was taken back a bit by his appearance, but after eight bars we knew we had an exceptional keyboard player and he got the job that night. We enjoyed him staying with us when he did, but we all knew it wouldn't last long, and we made the most of it.'

Through Simms, Rick was introduced to a likeable bass player called Chas Cronk, who was to join Rick's former group, the Strawbs, in 1973, and who has layed with them intermittently ever since. This meeting was to herald the start of one of the most fantastic session schedules ever known in the British music business. Many of the sessions – backing top musicians in the recording studio - took place while Rick was still a student, and in four frenetic years he was to do more than 2,000.

Chas still remembers that first meeting. 'Dave Simms used to tell me about this whiz kid he knew,' he said. 'Everyone in his band was really impressed with his talent. Rick and I met one day in the Musical Bargain   Centre and hit it off together - we knew each other's dirty jokes!

'I was doing some sessions with a member of the *Ike and Tina Turner Band* and I got Rick in on some of them. That was where he met record producers Denny Cordell and Tony Visconti, who were very impressed with his performance. And it went on from there. Once he got into a couple of proper sessions, his talent spoke for itself and there was no holding him. People were

---

* For those of you from outside the UK, a Geordie is someone who hails from the fair city of Newcastle-upon-Tyne in the North-East of England.

offering him work all over the place.'

And that is when the then virtually unknown David Bowie came into the picture.

Gus Dudgeon, who has since produced Elton John's big hits, (and who sadly died in 2002) recalls, 'Tony Visconti and I were then working in the same suite of offices.

In those days, you couldn't give Bowie away. The only record company that would take him was Mercury, in America. I knew Bowie from the days when I was an engineer at Decca and I did all the engineering on the two albums that he did for them.

One day Tony called me over the internal phone and said, "I know this sounds bizarre, Gus, but I've been working with David, and Mercury say he must record 'Space Oddity' as a single because the first American moon shot is coming up.

I want to do the album with him but I can't stand this song. Would you be interested?"

'I listened to the demo and thought it was unbelievable. I couldn't believe Tony didn't want to do it, and so I called him up and said I'd do it. This was in the early days of Mellotrons. I think *The Beatles'* 'Abbey Road' had come out by then and they had used it a lot on that album. So as Bowie and I were discussing it we came up with the idea of a Mellotron, not to be used as a string section, but as its typical sound - very doleful and mournful. We decided that was fine, but there weren't many people who knew how to get a decent sound out of the instrument. So we got the whole thing planned down to the smallest detail, because I knew 'Space Oddity' had a chance of being a hit. We planned where the Mellotron would come in and out, but because we knew so little we couldn't really write a part for it.

So then we went back to Tony's office, told him what we were going to do, and asked him if he knew anybody who could play a Mellotron. He said, "I only know one bloke, called Wakeman, but he plays in a dance band." I said sarcastically, "That sounds great." And he said, "He's all right. I've been using him on *Juniors Eyes** sessions." So I said, "Well, it's a gamble but let's give it a whirl. If it's a disaster we'll over-dub it again."

'So we went into Trident Studios, London, and started running it through. But there was no sign of our Mellotron player. I thought, "This is great!" We got to the point where we had the whole thing down to a fine art and it really was sounding good. I was feeling very pleased with myself because it was the first time that I had really worked on a record, and something that had sounded a certain way in my head was beginning to sound correct in the studio.

---

* *Junior's Eyes* were band from Hull, who made one LP 'Battersea Power Station' in 1969, and later worked as David Bowie's backing band on a BBC Radio session and a couple of other studio recordings.

'At the last minute the door opened and this great long streak walked in and said, "I'm terribly sorry. My name's Rick Wakeman - I've been booked to play Mellotron." So I said, "Well, this is a bit of an inopportune time to arrive. We're on the point of laying a track down." He said, "Gosh, I'm terribly sorry." I told him, "The only thing I can do is mark on this chart the points where I would like you to play, and maybe while we lay this one down you can sit and listen to the thing as a whole and see what is required. I must be honest with you, I know very little about Mellotrons - I don't know how to get a sound out of them or anything." Rick said, "Leave it to me."

'So I went over to the box and did a take and Rick sat there looking at his part without playing a note. Barry, the engineer, looked at me and raised his eyebrows as if to say, "Who's this freak?" And I said, "I don't know. Just some mad bloke that Visconti sent me."

Anyway, we got to the end of the first take and decided to have a playback, and Rick came in and listened to it. I reminded him again of the places and he said, "It's all right, I've worked it out. Are you going to do another take?" I said we were. He asked, "Do you mind if I have a go on this one?" I thought this was pretty ambitious but said, "All right."

'Well, we did a run-through and got three-quarters of the way through and Rick came in the right place. And what he played was exactly what I wanted. It was incredible! We did one more take and it was a master. I thought, "This is weird." This strange bloke was all covered in spots and had greasy hair, wearing the most dreadful clothes. And we were all wearing Carnaby Street stuff.

We sat down and listened to the playback and he said, "That's all right, isn't it?" I said. "It sounds pretty good to me. I think we have a hit there." And Rick said. "Well, is that all you want?" I said, "Yes, thanks very much." And off he went. Just like that, back to his ballroom job. I thought, "What a weird bloke!" I really liked him. I thought he was great. But he was so weird!"

Rick told me, 'I thought 'Space Oddity' was a guaranteed monster record. It came out around July 1970, and I played it to lots of people. Everybody said, "No, it's not very good." I thought after a while they must have been right, because it did nothing at all. But around Christmas it suddenly came to life again, and did monstrously well.'

The *Middlesex County Times*, Rick's local paper in Ealing, reported at the time:

> The higher David Bowie's record, 'Space Oddity', climbs the hit parade, the more excited Northolt pop musician, Ricky Wakeman, becomes.
>
> For twenty-year-old Ricky, who lives with his parents at Wood End Gardens, and is a former pupil of Drayton Manor Grammar School, is a "guest' musician on the record.
>
> 'I sit in on many recording sessions,' Ricky, who is 6 feet 2 inches, explained. 'On this record, made a week before the Americans landed on the moon, I played an instrument called a Mellotron. When the record was first released it did not catch on, but now it's really climbing the charts.'

In 1975, Bowie's space record did even better second time around - it reached No. 1 in the charts when it was re-released, but hardly anyone knew of Rick's contribution to its success.

How much did Wakeman get for his part in the record? 'All I got was a £9 session fee,' he said. 'But

that's what doing sessions was all about. You accepted that all you got was the session fee. There was no royalty if the disc was a hit.'

Another huge hit Wakeman played on in his hectic session days was 'Morning Has Broken', Cat Stevens's lovely version of the old hymn tune[*]. Rick was particularly proud of being involved with this song because of his religious beliefs. His beautiful piano playing is a highlight of the disc.

'Paul Samwell-Smith, the producer, and Cat Stevens (left) really weren't sure how the track was going to go, and we spent the whole day doing it,' said Rick. 'We brought it up from nothing and worked out different ways of doing it, working from a little old hymn book. I get a kick out of hearing both these records again, especially because they were sessions where I was allowed a bit of freedom to contribute what I wanted, not what either the musical director or the producer wanted me to play.'

Rick recalled those busy days. 'I was doing three or four sessions in twenty-four hours. I would finish one and then race off to the next, maybe at a studio on the other side of London. I started off at £9 for a full session and £6 for half a session, and over the years it went up to £15.

I particularly remember my first-ever session, where we did a great song called 'The Running Kind' which was never released. I've still got the copy master-tape at home.'

I asked Chas Cronk why he thought Wakeman did so many sessions. 'I don't think to start off with he saw himself playing with a band. And session work certainly gave him a lot of experience. But in the end I think he was doing more than he would have liked to have done because he was so popular and so much in demand. I guess he was trying to build a career for himself, anyway, so apart from the financial angle, just doing them was a good thing for him. Some sessions also gave him a chance to try his hand at arranging and he did quite a lot of that at the time. I think the sessions represented to him a way of getting quite a few facets of his musical ability out - not just playing but arranging for various instruments, including strings and brass. He was such a good musician and I thought, "What is a guy like this doing just working here, there and everywhere when he could be doing so much better?" But he was still at college, and I don't think at that time he had really decided where he was going. He was quite happy doing gigs all over the place.'

And, as usual with Rick, there were plenty of laughs along the way.

'He and his cars were always classics,' Chas remembers. 'He was quite an insane driver - I dare say he looks after his current cars more carefully - but I remember one night when we were going to Morgan

---

* Whereas 'Morning Has Broken' is a popular and well-known Christian hymn first published in 1931 with words by English author Eleanor Farjeon, it is set to a traditional Gaelic tune known as "Bunessan" (it shares this tune with the 19th Century Christmas Carol "Child in the Manger"

Studios to do a session. We stopped at the *Ace Café*, the rockers' haven on the North Circular Road, West London, and went in for a bacon sandwich. He drove the rest of the way round the North Circular steering with his knees, using his hands for the sandwich. I was terrified, but things like that never used to bother him. He was a good driver really, just a bit of a prankster with it.

'I remember another journey we made up to Leeds.' Chas went on. 'We were steaming up the M1 Motorway in Rick's Ford Cortina and after about forty miles we headed into a blizzard. Then we burst a tyre, but Rick didn't think much of it although the car was slewing all over the motorway. Luckily, we were on a clear a stretch, so we pulled over, got it changed and carried on up to Leeds. Coming back down the motorway in atrocious weather, we were hammering down the outside lane with snow beating down on all sides. Rick didn't take his foot off the throttle once. We hurtled along with headlights on and horn blaring, and near enough just knocked everything out of the way. About half-way down he suddenly realized we needed more petrol and as he took his foot off the accelerator to go up the slip road, the replacement tyre we had put on just blew right out. There must have been a foot-long gash right round it.

We limped up into the service station and I the guy asked, "How fast have you been going?" Apparently it was lucky we didn't slow down before, or it would have blown on the motorway. Rick had been aquaplaning all the way down because the road was so wet. But he didn't seem to worry too much about it. With anyone else I would have been genuinely scared. But it was fun all the time with Rick. He just used to kill himself laughing and have another pint.

'Beer. curries and music were the things at the time. If we went somewhere for a drink, we would go out and have a curry. There was an Indian restaurant in Harrow which became a favourite. We made friends with the manager, who used to make the curries hotter every time, so eventually we crawled out with sweat pouring off us. Rick likes his curries hot, anyway. But the manager used to take great delight in watching us ease our way panting out of the door.'

Chas remembers the serious side, too. 'I don't think I know anyone in the music business who has worked as hard as Rick has done. He just has such a brilliant talent. And the best thing about him as a musician for me was that he was one of those people who could bring the best out of someone else. When I did sessions for him when he did some film music for *Zee and Co.* a few years ago, he would put very difficult bass runs in and I would say, "I can't play that, Rick." And his confidence was so great that he would say, "Of course you can Chas, don't worry." And funnily enough, you could do it. If you were doing a session for somebody else you would be horrified by something like that and you wouldn't be able to do it. Looking back over a career, Rick has been one of the people who has been able to provide a spark for me. He has so much energy, he distributes it all over the place. And he inspires confidence everywhere.'

And through the sessions, Rick discovered something vital to his future. "I found that when they put the music in front of me I could not only play the notes through the training I had, but I could give something, too. I could add little extra things or embellish or alter parts, which were to the producer's liking. I knew instantly that was my forte. I'd found I could give and take. And in a strange way, that was the missing link in my life. That was the hardest thing to find, and I found it through the sessions. Ironically there are lots of stories about people who believe in God. Normally, that's their last missing link; for me strangely enough, that was the link I had in the beginning, and the sessions were the link to what I was meant to do in my life.'

The man who played the biggest role in Rick's session career, was David Katz, one of Britain's top 'fixers', though he prefers to be called an orchestral contractor. There are about twelve top fixers in Britain and they handle most of the sessions around. Producers phone them up and the fixers find out who is available. The fixer pays musicians for the session - and usually ends up getting ten per cent of the total cost of the musicians.

Wakeman and Katz met via Gus Dudgeon. 'I remember David Katz spoke to me the day after I had done a session with Rick and he had been brilliant,' said Gus. 'And I said to David: "Have you any gigs for a good pianist?" "Yes, I'm getting calls for pianists all the time. A good young pianist who can do sessions and can read is very hard to find." And I said: "Well I know a guy who is really amazing. He can read and he can play anything. I don't know what his abilities are like at contributing something totally original, but if someone says to him, 'Can you play like Fats Waller or Jerry Lee Lewis?' or anyone else, this kid can do it." So I gave David, Rick's name and number and I didn't hear anything more about it.

'Then I rang David about three months later and he said: "That bloke you sent me is unbelievable. Everybody rings up for him." I was so pleased. Rick was fantastic for him. Because Rick could be sent on any gig - it didn't matter what kind of session or who booked it. Rick was doing an incredible amount of sessions at one time. It was insane. He would rush from one session to another.'

I asked Gus if he thought Wakeman was silly taking on so much work in those early days. 'Everybody's got to live,' he said, 'It's very difficult to survive as just a straightforward session musician and still maintain some kind of musical integrity. Because you have to prostitute your art, you have to do terrible sessions a lot of the time. In fact eighty-five per cent of the time you have to do awful sessions and then occasionally you get a good one. I'm afraid that is the way the session musician's syndrome works. I think it's a shame because it destroys a lot of musicians. I also think it possibly makes a lot of musicians. I think it probably made Rick, it gave him the incentive to say: "This is great but what am I learning from it? I really must break away from it and get on with something of my own." I don't think it was silly for him to do so much work. I think it was probably a good thing. I'm sure he learned a hell of a lot from it.'

Katz turned out to be a charming man who looks upon himself as the Hughie Green[*] of the music business. 'I like giving people the opportunity,' he told me. 'I put Rick on sessions and we got on fine. I like him so much, and soon he became my number-one piano player. After about a year, I got people who said they wanted the fellow with the long hair".'

Among the sessions Rick did for Katz was playing on themes for hit television series such as 'The Avengers' and 'Jason King'.

Katz described Rick as a very generous musician. 'Generous I mean in the sense that on the session he was in, he would never hold anything back. His contribution was absolutely wonderful. He never, from the moment he sat down at the beginning of the sessions, stopped contributing towards it, creating and re-creating all the time. He was a paragon of how a studio musician or any musician should behave.'

Rick became known in the business as 'One-take Wakeman'. The sessions came pouring in for David Bowie, *White Plains, Edison Lighthouse, Brotherhood of Man, T. Rex,* Cilla Black and Mary Hopkin -

---

[*] Whilst younger readers will have never heard of him, those readers of a certain age will remember TV Personality and Game Show host Hughie Green, who died at the age of 77 in 1997. He was best known for being host of the popular TV talent show *Opportunity Knocks.*

to name only a few. Then came the album work with Elton John, Al Stewart, Ralph MacTell, Cat Stevens, *Magna Carta*, *Black Sabbath*, Dana, Clive Dunn and Kenny Lynch. One session Wakeman particularly enjoyed playing on was for John Williams, the prince of the classical guitar. Wakeman's keyboards were used on Williams's beautiful album 'Changes' and joining him on this unusual experimental record, which was a showpiece of all the different sounds that Williams wanted around his guitar, were some of the finest names in rock - Madeline Bell, Herbie Flowers, Terry Cox and Danny Thompson.

'Like myself, John Williams was trained at the Royal College of Music, though he was there before me,' said Rick. 'And I think he made a better success of his time there than I did.'

Rick, on the piano and organ, later joined Australian-born Williams and his rock friends on the stage of the Royal Festival Hall for an Easter Monday charity show for War on Want.

When he wasn't doing sessions, Rick had yet another job; playing organ with the Ronnie Smith band at the Top Rank Ballroom, Watford. This didn't last long as Rick got the sack for playing the goat instead of the keys. But he was to go back to the band later when they moved to Reading.

With all these new interests it was hardly surprising Rick decided that a teacher's course, which meant he would be ramming music down the throats of uninterested children, was also not for him.

He takes up the story of why he finally quit the Royal College of Music: 'It was ironical - the college couldn't and wouldn't throw me out, because I'd passed the end of term exams, but they wanted me to leave. So the only thing I had to do was to find some excuse. The only way I could get out was literally not turn up, so I took sessions whenever I could. I told the professors I would not be coming anymore.'

And so he said goodbye to the illustrious college, exactly half-way through his course, and headed towards the East End to explain his decision to his father. 'I've learnt a lot there,' he told his dumbstruck father, 'but I've learnt as well that I could never stand up in front of a class of

children insisting that they learn music that half of them aren't interested in. And if you're not interested in music it's useless. I've found what I want to do - compose and play rock music.' His father knew it was a horrific gamble, and was very disappointed. 'Dad had kept telling his friends that I was at the Royal College - it was like saying I was at Oxford - and it wasn't going to be easy to tell them I had dropped out to try and become a rock-and-roll star,' said Rick. 'I was really upset for my dad.' His mother was even more put out - she cried all afternoon. But Mrs Wakeman finally wiped away the tears and in characteristic style told Rick as he hiked in through the door, a student no more. 'Well you're not going to stay around here doing nothing while I go out to work. Get yourself a job!'

Although Wakeman knew he was already a successful session musician he longed for his technique to be even better, so he continued his music lessons with Mrs Symes. They paid handsome dividends.

'Because of the many sessions and outside engagements he had, Richard would arrive home in the early hours and would be in a deep sleep in the mornings when he was due to attend my 10:00am. lesson,' said Mrs Symes. 'Some occasions I rang his next-door neighbour to wake him. She would throw lumps of earth at his bedroom window but usually this didn't wake him. So then she had to get a long clothes pole which she tapped at his window until the sleeping beauty awoke. He would finally turn up for his lesson an hour or so late and usually with a hangover.'

FOUR
Just Want to be Your Teddy Bear

W ould you like to win a teddy bear?' asked the dark-haired girl wearing a green and white skirt and blouse, a dicky bow and a sash saying: 'Drink Shloer Apple Juice'.

Rick was a bit taken aback as he walked into the Top Rank Ballroom, Reading. 'What do I want a teddy bear for?' he asked.

'Well,' she replied with a cheeky smile. 'You could give it to me.'

Rick had got a job with the Ronnie Smith dance band, his first steady work since leaving the Royal College, in the Berkshire town, 30 miles out of London, and famous only for its biscuits and struggling soccer team.

It was different from Rick's day-time work on the sessions where he was playing with some of Britain's top musicians. At the smoky ballroom each night he was churning out the latest teenybopper pop hits to an audience who basically preferred the records anyway and had gone there for a good night out, a chance to pick up a girl or guy, and down a few drinks. And as far as the band were concerned, they too wanted to pick as many girls as possible in between pints.

Ros Woolford - eventually to become the first Mrs Rick Wakeman - a petite brunette from a nearby council estate recalls that meeting. 'I thought Rick was enormously tall. His blond hair was very long for the period and he was only allowed in because he was a musician. The bouncers threw out anyone else who had hair that went over their collar. And Rick was a gaudy dresser. He had a really nice jacket, but instead of it being a normal colour, it was covered with turquoise-blue flowers and he wore it with a really thick silk shirt. It was his best and only gear at the time.

'That night Rick had come to take away the Hammond Organ as the band had an outside function to do in Wembley the following day. I was doing an apple juice promotion at the front entrance. Later I was carrying some bottles on a tray and he walked straight into me and knocked them all on to the floor. He made quite an impression on me one way and another!

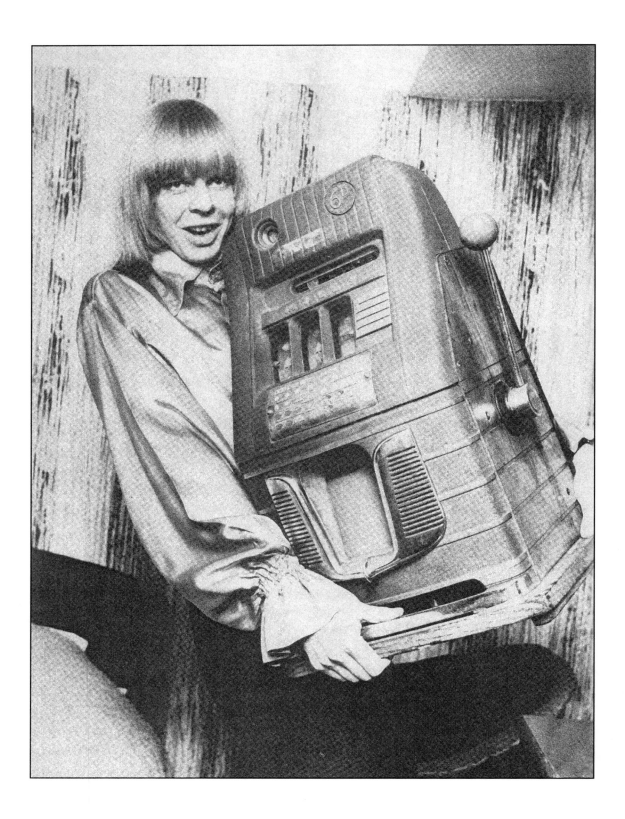

'When I ran out of juice, the manager said I could leave and I went upstairs to the bar. Rick had already offered to buy me a drink to make up for the accident, and there were two blokes there, one I'd been out with the night before, and Rick.

I think Rick intrigued me with his old clothes and cheeky manner, so I chose him.

'Rick took me home that night in a friend's van - he was Colin Spiers, who was later best man at our wedding – and soon we started going out regularly. I liked Rick because he made me laugh a lot, but I cringed the night he met my parents. As we watched Rick walk up the path in his jumble-sale clothes, my mum said, "Oh Ros, you get worse. What's that?" I said: "That's Rick." And my dad came in and added: "What the . . . is that?" Dad took Rick into the front room and started cross-examining him. "Why have you got such long hair?" he said. "Why have you got such short hair?" countered Rick in his usual tactful manner.

'"I asked you first," said Dad. "Well, I'd look daft with short back and sides on stage, wouldn't I?" Rick asked him. "And you'd look silly at work with long hair." Dad thought that was a fair answer.

'We got engaged after three months. Rick proposed to me in the car outside Mrs. Symes's house after giving me a guided tour of his early childhood.

'We used to spend ages "talking" in the car. He would say he was going to have lots of money, a big house and a nice car, and he really meant it. I don't know if I believed him, but I didn't disbelieve him. I didn't know if he played the piano well or not. I always thought he was quite good because people told me he was.'

Rick's romance soon appeared in his local paper, the *Middlesex County Times*, Ealing. He told a reporter how he had given Ros an important choice to make. 'If you marry me, you must accept my one-armed bandit in the bedroom as well,' he told her.

The story read:

> When attractive Rosaline Woolford marries Northolt pop star, Ricky Wakeman, later this month, she will not be gaining just a husband, but a one-armed bandit as well.
>
> For 20-year-old Ricky, of Wood End Gardens, Northolt, is insisting his one-armed bandit stays. 'I've had it about twelve months now,' said Ricky, a former pupil of Drayton Manor Grammar School, Hanwell. 'I keep it in my bedroom.' He added: 'I think Rosaline gets more fun from it than I do, so I don't really think she will really mind it joining us.'
>
> Ricky claims his one-armed bandit had helped him save. 'On occasions I have emptied it and have been able to take between £8 and £9 to the bank,' he said.

Ros reluctantly agreed and the rather silly story about Rick's demand was carried along with a picture of a smirking Wakeman affectionately holding his one-armed bandit.

It was his second Press appearance. The first was about his session on Bowie's 'Space Oddity', for the same paper.

The big day, 28th March 1970, was really one to remember, especially from Rick's point of view. 'The

wedding in Reading, was hysterical, it was like a giant brewery convention,' he recalls. 'Everybody was drunk. I think the highlight of the evening was when my mum came over to me while I was talking to my mates and said: "I think you'd better be making your way home now, Richard. It's seventy miles and Ros will be very tired. She wants to get a good night's sleep. Get her straight to bed." Dad had to take her on one side as we collapsed in laughter. The local Reading paper headlined the wedding as: "Easter Bride Rosaline marries her pop star."'

When Rick went to Reading, he started his second spell with Ronnie Smith's (opposite) band. He met Smith for the first time when he went with a friend, Graham Turner, who was repairing a Hammond Organ, to the Watford Top Rank Ballroom, where the band was playing at the time. Rick had never played a Hammond before and was looking forward to trying one out.

'My friend asked if I would like to go along as his "tester". He said nobody but the manager would be there and it would be all right. My eyes lit up because Hammonds were to me like Rolls-Royces. And it was their biggest and best model that I was to "test". I was taken aback by the size of the ballroom and even more by the size and tone of this incredible organ. I was playing away to my heart's content when Ronnie came in.

'He looked very severe and said, "What are you doing on this organ?" My friend told him I was testing it. So he asked me if I could read music and put a sheet in front of me. I played it and he was a bit taken back. So he asked me if I played the piano and when he heard me he offered me a job. It was £12 a week plus a free uniform, starting the next night.

'I was amazed how easily I had got the job, but I was brought down to earth a bit when my mum rushed me off to the hairdressers. She wanted me to look smart, but I finished up looking as if a pudding basin had been shoved on my head, and what made it worse was she made me put on this horrific suit for my first night. It was like an Oxfam reject - I think they'd turned it down twice.'

Ashley Holt, who sang on *Journey to the Centre of the Earth* and later joined Rick's band was then with Ronnie Smith's band and remembers the night Rick turned up. 'This petrified guy arrived in a grey suit, white shirt and black tie - an amazing sight because he was more than 6 feet tall. He really looked young. I said to Ronnie, "What the hell's this? You've got to be kidding." But I discovered later his mother had sent him out religiously in a suit because it was his first date with us. My comments almost reduced him to tears, but then he sat down at the organ and played and it was the most amazing thing I have ever heard. He may not have looked trendy, but what great music he produced that night.

'To start with Rick did very well, but the big functions the band played at were his downfall. They were very lahdee dah,' Ashley remembers. 'Organizations like British Airways would hire us and Rick would have to play foxtrots and quicksteps. Once he'd been with the band a while, he wouldn't turn the parts up and used to improvise over them. Ronnie often wouldn't let me on stage because I was a hooligan and just wanted to rock and roll, and Rick went the same way.

'When it came to his solo Rick often didn't know where he was on the arrangement and he would just busk. We always used to laugh because Ronnie would tell him off in the corridor afterwards. He used to say, "I see you played that solo really well again Rick. Pity you didn't have the right part up, it would have gone ten times better." We used to look forward to Thursdays, Saturdays and Sundays, which were rock-and-roll and soul nights.'

Then the band moved to Reading, and Rick says he got the sack for his misbehaviour at the functions. But the musical break did not last long and Ronnie took Rick back on condition he would take the job seriously. He rejoined as soon as he left the Royal College of Music.

They were tough days, but looking back now, Wakeman remembers them also as funny times. 'It was a dangerous occupation because of the gang fights that often took place, especially on Saturday nights, which we called "dodge the beer glass night". You could always sense when there was going to be trouble. The rival mobs used to get on opposite sides of the dance floor. When it started, Ronnie would get the revolving stage to swing round and we would be ducking as the glasses went flying. Ronnie would continue conducting and act as if nothing was happening and say in the same tone: "See you all again next week."'

Ashley says it was terrifying. 'There would be a hail of glasses on the stage. One night I saw a guy try to hit someone over the head with a table with a tubular frame. Luckily, the legs got caught in the acoustic tiling and that just stopped him from crowning the guy.

'They would chase each other into the toilets with pint mugs ready to clout each other. The crazy thing was that as long as you had a shirt and tie on they'd let you in. You could have been well behaved and tie-less and you'd have been barred.'

The band had their own uniform, 'The cloth was like a "horsehair blanket"' Ashley remembers. 'I think a few of the band resented me, because as lead singer I could wear frilly shirts and kaftans. But Rick had to wear this awful jacket. It was so old and moth-eaten, he said the first time he put it on, Arkle the racehorse fell out! The pockets were even sealed so we couldn't leave fag ends. Having long arms he'd find a jacket that was the right length to the waist but the arms would come up to his elbow, and where the sleeve finished, his arms looked like long lanky pork sausages sticking out of the end. Thank God he never supplied trousers. The coats were orange and aquamarine green with RS on the pockets and they were worn with bootlace ties. Band members always hoped someone would leave so they could get a jacket that fitted better.'

The disc jockey often suffered from the humour of Rick and Ashley. 'He was on the other side of the revolving stage and we used to put our hands through and grab his leg when he tried to walk by to get to his record decks. There was lots of gagging going on. Then he would decide his time was up and would swing the stage without us all realizing it was our turn. The band would often arrive with half of them still with one arm in their jackets trying to get their music ready.'

Mrs. Wakeman was rather worried at first by some of Rick's new-found friends in the "music business'. And Ashley was number one on her list of dubious characters.

Ashley recalls: 'I used to pick Rick up for rehearsals and the first time I went I knocked on the door and she just couldn't believe it when she saw me. She shouted out: "Richard, it's one of your long-haired things at the door." Now they are the best friends. Rick's long hair was a constant source of embarrassment to his mother. One day after a blazing row over it, Rick packed his suitcase and left home. He was soon back, however.'

Rick and Ashley often relieved the tedium for the band with their little tricks. 'I remember Rick used to balance little batteries on the keys and would not be there for about forty-eight bars - he'd gone off to the toilet. And you'd turn round and nothing had changed. It still sounded the same, as if he was holding the block chord down.

'He used a nylon wheel off a lighting gantry to run up and down the keyboard, and he'd rock the organ and made the reverberation unit crash. Rick was into the showman bit, especially when he'd had a few drinks. He used to walk round the other side of the organ and play over the top. We were going to turn it on end one night, but Ronnie threatened us with the sack.'

Rick said a lot of musicians told him that working in this type of band was the kiss of death.

Commented Rick: 'Ronnie was a character and he taught me a lot about life and I'm sure if everybody who worked with him were honest they really would admit they had a good time. I think this must be true, judging by the number of stories musicians tell about him.'

I managed to track down the now almost legendary Ronnie Smith and found he has now given up his 'Top of the Pops' dance band and is finding success as a jazz musician, much in demand for sessions. Ronnie, also a film extra with parts in films like *Chitty Chitty Bang Bang*, *Cromwell* and *The Devils*, told me of those early days with the spotty Rick Wakeman.

'Rick would drive me to despair some nights. He was then using my prized £2,500, A100 Hammond and did all sorts of outrageous things to it. His main trick was to run a paint roller up and down the keys and also rock it backwards and forwards to rock the reverb. That produced a really freaky sound. I used to yell at him, "Rick, treat my organ with respect." Rick had a way of inspiring the others in the band to unknown heights, but he also caused me nightmares because something would get out of control. We were only supposed to play "Top of the Pops" and not get into heavy rock. If we did, I got a rocket from the management'

Ronnie says that Rick found the functions a real cross to bear. 'He was playing waltzes and foxtrots and his technique was just too good to be confined in that strict type of music. His talent was of giant proportions, but it was having to be crushed into the simple arrangements of dance music. I hated having to tell him "Keep it simple, Rick", but if I didn't, I knew I'd get into real trouble with the manager who was invariably peering over the balcony at us.

'Rick never served in the Army, but this dance-band experience was a bit like a musical national service. Not too pleasant, but vital as a character-building exercise.'

Watching a musician of Wakeman's ability, recalled Ronnie Smith, terrified him. 'What he could do on a keyboard was beyond me,' he confessed. 'I used to yell at him about using the paint roller, but I've now managed to get hold of it and I use it myself. He taught me a tremendous lot. In fact, I know that Rick is now the model for all up-and-coming keyboard players. He's a leader and others follow.'

I saw the famous paint roller Rick used when he was receiving the dazzling salary of £24 a week with the Smith band. I am sure he would not begrudge Ronnie now using this early Wakeman weapon.

With all this lunacy going on, it was hardly surprising that Ronnie sacked Rick for the second time. 'In his own way he was probably right both times to get rid of me,' says Rick. But Ashley disputes that: 'I used to say to Ronnie, "I know Rick's going to make it. I know he's going to be a star. Why let him go if he wants to play?" Ronnie used to say: "No, no, we don't need him."'

Ronnie told me: 'Rick often said he was going to become a big rock star and that one day he'd make it. I believed him. It was obvious. Talent was just pouring out of him. When he left, the band somehow went flat. And when Ashley left as well, we were never the same again.'

So another chapter in Wakeman's colourful life was over and another was about to unfold - and as usual it began in a pub.

FIVE

Salvador Dali – Who's He?

Paris in the spring is a great place for a honeymoon by anybody's standards. And for Rick there was not just the excitement of a new life with Ros, but also a whole new musical career that began to unfold under a French big top.

That life-changing trip to Paris was the result of a phone call from Dave Cousins, a one-time bluegrass banjo picker and founder of the *Strawberry Hill Boys*, later to become the *Strawbs*.

Rick had done sessions with the then-struggling group and played on their 'Dragonfly' album, as well as on numerous BBC radio folk programmes. 'Dragonfly' was the first time his name appeared on an L.P. sleeve and he wrote and thanked Cousins, saying how delighted he was to see his name in print.

Cousins rang him up and they arranged to have a 'few jars' in the *Greenwood* pub in Greenford, Middlesex. 'What are you doing these days?' Cousins asked him. 'I've left Reading and I'm working with a group called *Spinning Wheel* in the Greyhound at Ilford. I get paid £40 a week for seven nights and Sunday lunchtime,' said Rick.

Cousins recalls: 'A brilliant idea suddenly struck me, and I said, "Do you want to come and play with us?" He sort of shook with delight. He was really emotional. And he said, "God that's fantastic. I'd really love to."

'I told him, "We can only pay you £25 a week. It's a bit of a drop. But we're going to Paris next week." He said, "But I'm getting married next week." And I told him, "Well you can turn it into your honeymoon." Before we went to Paris we did a TV show in Manchester. Ralph McTell, who was also on the show, said, "He's exceptional isn't he? When does he join you?" And I said, "He has joined. We're off to France next week."'

This offer plucked Rick away from the spit and sawdust atmosphere of a smoky Ilford pub, where his world revolved around beer, darts and blue poems.

Rick had moved from his beloved Northolt to Ilford, Essex, where he and Ros shared a poky little flat.

He had got the job with *Spinning Wheel* through answering an advertisement in the *Melody Maker*. He was shocked to find he had to go for an audition first but sailed through the test and began his nightly stint of penetrating the alcoholic haze with the group's music. The highlight of his spell with *Spinning Wheel* was his new-found talent as a man of letters. Not exactly a William Wordsworth, however, but writing blue poems with blue hands in a freezing outside toilet at his flat.

'To boost attendances at the pub we used to include little funny sketches and the poems I wrote in the loo to keep the circulation going in my hands. They were a bit near the mark though,' said Rick. 'But the customers used to love them.'

Recalls a blushing Ros: 'The poems were really great, but really rude. "Dark Blue" you could call them.'

At first Rick was happy playing in front of a live audience instead of for a record producer behind a glass panel, but then he became tired of entertaining the same beery audience each night. 'When I was offered the chance to join the *Strawbs* I thought this would be the opportunity to play in front of new people each night. And I thought - and still do - that Dave Cousins is most probably the best lyricist of his century, musically. I thought he wrote incredibly nice melodies - but I didn't think the way they were treated was very good.

'This went back to the give and take thing. I could take an awful lot from his words and music and perhaps add a bit as well. That was my "give" part. That's why I joined.'

Rick was given his chance to join the *Strawbs* by Mr Bob Wheatley, who despite having Rick contracted at Ilford, did not stand in his way.

Dave Cousins, a mathematics graduate from Leicester University, started his career singing Rambling Jack Elliott type of songs, but he became more and more influenced by traditional English folk music, an influence which has stayed with him. Then Cousins heard banjo playing in Lester Scruggs style and he started to learn it. He met up with Tony Hooper, a slight youth with tangled hair, and the duo toured the folk clubs as David and Anthony, a name that Cousins and Hooper now try and live down. Then they switched to bluegrass and called themselves the *Strawberry Hill Boys*. Sandy Denny (of *Fairport Connection* and *Fotheringay* fame) joined them, and they moved back into folk. That combination did not last long, although during that time they produced an album in Denmark called 'All Our Own Work', which was re-released in 1973, on the Pickwick label. Cousins tried new sounds with electric bass and cello, and several different musicians. The cello began to dominate their work with a loss of inventiveness, and they badly needed to try something new. For the album 'Dragonfly' Rick was given some sessions and immediately struck up a friendship with Cousins, who recognized immediately that here was a musician of extraordinary talent. Strangely enough Dave Cousins did not at first use Rick on the organ in the group.

'We intended to just stay an acoustic group - two acoustic guitars, bass and piano, and go round the folk clubs and do radio programmes.'

But the trip to Paris was not like that at all. It was a rock-and-roll circus with bands backing the acts! Rick at that time did not have any keyboards, so he borrowed an organ and electric piano from another band.

'The *Strawbs* were a pretty gentle act, so we backed the child jugglers and the guy who walked the tightrope. When they reached the climax, our music had to reach a climax. When the tightrope walker did a forward roll I had to stand there and flutter an imitation drum roll, because we didn't have any drums,' said Rick.

One night there was a special guest at the circus - no less than Salvador Dali, the renowned Spanish surrealist painter. But when the great man was called on stage to take a bow, Rick was not quite sure what was going on.

"Suddenly, this old man with a moustache came on with a walking stick. He could have been a road sweeper for all I cared, so I shouted things like, "Kindly get off the stage", and "What are you doing up there waving your stick?" and "Please walk away in short jerky movements." We just went into the next number. Dave knew who he was, and said, "That's Salvador Dali." I said, "I don't care if he's Harold Wilson." I didn't know who he was. I thought, "Silly old sod, coming on the stage waving his stick.""

One of the group's first British dates was in Stoke with Roy Harper. 'They told us half the audience had come to see the Strawbs and we were delighted,' said Rick. The only snag was that "half the audience" amounted to about eight people.'

There was a much bigger turnout for another show with Harper at Birmingham Town Hall. A music critic for the *Melody Maker* wrote:

> The evening got off to a good start with the talented and versatile *Strawbs*, whose five members between them played dulcimer, sitar and various percussion instruments, as well as the more usual guitars, piano, organ and electric bass. I was particularly impressed by Rick Wakeman's solo contribution at the piano, used three days previously here by Count Basie. Mainly a straight piano number, this unnamed composition

(eventually entitled 'Temperament of Mind'), ranged through Griegish passages and a stomping blues; Rick's organ was mercifully restrained in volume; in fact the whole group impressed with their moderation in the use of volume, except perhaps for Dave Cousins's solid guitar; the acoustic guitars and other sounds were delightful.

After another show in Portsmouth, the local paper critic wrote: 'On this showing, the *Strawbs* defy any criticism. All they need is a bit of help from the public to put them where they rightfully belong.'

Rick recalls: 'We got the tag of being the first folk-rock band, and we used to drive to the concerts in a Humber Super Snipe, which later changed to a hired Transit, complete with a freelance roadie who worked also for a group called *Forever More*, and finally to a Mercedes Truck with seating even for the band. One night there was a unique bill at a college in Twickenham. The *Strawbs* headlined it with *Steeleye Span* and *Lindisfarne*. About 100 turned up for that one.'

A popular feature of later *Strawbs* performances was Rick's solo piano piece, which he called 'Temperament of Mind'. It started with a power failure. And it was to lead to him becoming too big a power in the group.

Rick remembers, "We were playing at Sheffield University, when all the electricity went off on stage. Dave, who at his best is one of the best stage talkers in the world, shouted out, "I'm glad this has happened now, because it's time for Rick's acoustic piano solo. Over to you Rick." I said I didn't know any music I could play. "You do now," he grimaced. So I played the first thing that came into my mind and just went rambling on until the power came back.' This unplanned solo soon became a regular highlight of *Strawbs* concerts.

'I called it 'Temperament of Mind' because I kept certain little phrases all the time, but I used to play it according to how I felt.'

And that piano solo led to an astonishing standing ovation at Rick's first big concert with the *Strawbs* at the Queen Elizabeth Hall, London, on 11th July 1970. The line-up for that concert, which was recorded 'live' by A&M Records, was Dave Cousins (opposite), Tony Hooper, Rick and two more new boys, Richard Hudson and John Ford, later to become the hit pop duo - Hudson-Ford. They had joined the *Strawbs* from the loud and violent *Elmer Gantry's Velvet Opera*. To many friends who had never heard them play, Rick was just an amiable loon, but when they heard him play at that concert they just could not believe their ears. In fact, the whole hall quickly realized here was a giant new talent that was greatly going to influence rock music.

And when Wakeman played 'Temperament of Mind' on the grand piano at the Queen Elizabeth Hall, and later a wild organ solo on 'Where is This Dream of Your Youth' the audience just exploded. He produced musical figures as yet unacceptable to folk-rock, including using the explosion of the built-in reverb by generally pushing the organ all over the stage. Ronnie Smith would have fainted at his behaviour.

Next morning the critics raved about the concert, and especially about the blond-haired keyboard man who had taken the show by storm.

In *The Times*, Michael Wale said: 'It can immediately be said that Wakeman is the instrumentalist pop find of the year. He is highly accomplished on piano, organ and harpsichord. Like the rest of the group he also has a sense of humour, as when he played solo – 'Temperament of Mind', ranging from classical, through silent movie accompaniments, to jazz. The applause with which the audience rewarded him was instant proof that a different sort of hero has been found.'

The other *Times* - the underground *International Times* - said: 'Rick Waterman [sic] is a near genius. His solo spot consisted of a mad jumble of horror themes, TV jingles and harpsichord and organ playing were equally effective. And his influence on the group is obviously quite considerable. They got three encores and they more than deserved them.'

Melody Maker's critic wrote: 'Watch out for Rick Wakeman. He has a near mastery of the keyboard. The capacity audience sat motionless as he wrestled with the organ flooding the hall with a torrent of sound. When he turned his attention to the piano, it was equally effective. Finally, he produced some of the best harpsichord rock I have yet heard.'

Rick could hardly believe the notices, because up to then his Press appearances had been limited to paragraphs in local papers. Now, overnight, he had become a national pop figure.

But the ultimate accolade - the biggest break of Rick's career - came shortly afterwards when a giant picture of Wakeman filled the front page of the *Melody Maker* with the heading 'Tomorrow's Superstar?' The article said: 'This is the man Keith Emerson hired a box at London's Lyceum to hear. Since the twenty-one-year-old keyboard virtuoso joined the group along with Ford and Hudson, they've evolved into one of the most exciting bands of the folk-rock scene.'

Dave Cousins said at the time: 'We were a machine that needed oiling – we were a folk group attracting a wider audience. Then when the others joined, it happened virtually overnight.'

Gus Dudgeon recalls that the picture was the turning point in Rick's career. 'I don't know who was responsible for that picture-story, but I reckon that front page in *Melody Maker* did more for Rick's career, possibly, than anything else before. As a musician he was already well proven but that doesn't mean a thing to kids who buy albums. Unless that person is attempting to make some kind of career of their own it doesn't matter how well known they are on album tracks.'

Now for the first time Rick's name was on the lips of rock fans all over the country, and when the live recording of the concert was released by A&M under the title of 'Just a Collection of Antiques and Curios' it immediately went into the charts. The title came from a line in the *Strawbs* 'Antique Suite', which consisted of four songs, and the idea of the suite occurred to *Dave Cousins* after he went to an old doctor's house in Southall, Middlesex, to see his collection of curios. In the corner of a large room was a pile of what seemed to be junk. In it Cousins found relics from the old man's life, objects that meant very little to anyone else, but were full of life and history for the aged doctor.

The song was about an elderly man dying in his living-room. As he dies, he looks around him and in every ornament and piece of furniture in his room a little bit of his past comes to life. A half-written letter to the wife who left him so many years ago floats from his lap on to the floor as the Grim Reaper comes to escort him away.

Cousins said: 'I tried to put myself in the place of the man dying in the room he always had known. When you die you are supposed to see the whole of your life flashing past you in one brief second. I was trying to think what this must have been like.

'The suite gave us a title and a sleeve for the album. The sleeve features pictures of personal relics of the people in the band, things like old toys, a football and a pipe. The setting of the pictures is something like a still life by an old master. The background is very musty. It's a highly personal sleeve; there's a little bit of each of us on it.'

'A little bit of each of us' sums it up. Anyone who has seen the *Strawbs* will know that they are one of those bands that believe in giving themselves completely to the audience.

The critics were ecstatic about the 'live' album produced and recorded by Tony Visconti. One wrote: '*Strawbs* deliver a certain beautiful blend of romance and nostalgia at times almost Elizabethan with that tinkling then strutting chord-phrasing. It's befitting that this album was recorded live at the Queen Elizabeth Hall, for it's there that Rick Wakeman's harpsichord work sounds well at home. ...Wakeman's 'Temperament of Mind', a neurotic five minutes on the piano - from classics to honky-tonk and Buster Keaton chases - adds a highly talented length of fun. In all, the best live recording I've ever heard.'

Michael Wale selected 'Antiques and Curios' as one of the best records of 1970 in a column in the *Financial Times*. He wrote: 'If there was a group that proved to be the find of 1970, then it was the *Strawbs,* who threw off their folk background and produced in a concert at the Queen Elizabeth Hall new music, well played, especially by Richard Hudson on drums and Rick Wakeman on organ.'

And the *Strawbs* even got a mention in *Rolling Stone*, the top American rock paper. But Rick was not too pleased with this one - they called him ROCK WANKMAN ....

The publicity also solved a solvency problem for Rick and Ros. Their bank manager demanded that they come to see him about their small overdraft, but before they arrived he read the rave report in *The Times*, and realized that cash would soon be no problem to this up-and-coming musician, and the overdraft stayed.

Round about the same time Rick went back to his old school and met his old music teacher, Mr Herrera, who obviously remembered the ten-shilling bet that helped get Rick to college. 'Where's the Rolls-Royce?' he asked. 'They just wouldn't believe I was still poor,' said Rick.

And back in Reading at the Top Rank Suite, Rick's new-found fame caused a few titters backstage. For a member of the band cut out the *Melody Maker* front page and pinned it up with the inscription: 'This man was sacked by Ronnie Smith. Tomorrow it could be you.'

SIX

Hangman and the Paint Roller

D ave Cousins could have willingly strung Rick up the night the *Strawbs* made their debut on *Top of the Pops*, the big audience BBC TV show. For by now they were a top group with promoters clamouring for their services.

'I remember that night vividly,' says Rick. 'We actually got on *TOTP* – and it's most probably the last time that I shall ever appear on that programme. They had what they called their album spot, which was the part of the show where all the teenyboppers could go out for a wee wee. I used to use my paint roller to play the organ solo on a track called 'Sheep', and it was my pride and joy. That night we were playing the 'Hangman and the Papist', which is a very powerful and meaningful number. And half-way through there was suddenly a shot of me standing there with the paint roller. It didn't go down too well with Dave.'

Cousins remembers: 'It was one of my most serious songs, and the paint roller totally destroyed its whole symbolism. All because of this silly lone bugger with a paint roller. After I rounded on him and said. "What the hell did you do that for?" He replied, "It's my gimmick isn't it?" I told him, "Thanks very much, you destroyed the song." And he said, "Oh, I didn't mean to." Things like that endear you to him.'

Rick had other gimmicks in those days - including a block of wood with holes for screws which held down various big chords on the lower manual keyboard of his organ, so he could play solos over the top on other instruments. The showman in him was really coming out at each gig with the *Strawbs*. He would rock his organ wildly and grimace as if in agony as he played and his long solos became more and more exciting as Rick went through his act, after leaving the rest of the group out in the cold.

Rick was becoming more and more of a 'name'. He was a new hero for the Press to latch on to. *The Sunday Mirror* called him to be photographed along with Ros - in a second-hand boiler suit at the King's Road shop in Chelsea which specialized in selling denims and dungarees. They were second-hand with genuine holes, and preferably with the previous wearer's name on the pocket. Rick paid £6 for his cast-offs at the shop. The paper featured Rick sporting his dungarees, with his arm round Ros, in her boiler suit.

Gus Dudgeon bumped into Rick shortly afterwards and recalls the incident. 'Rick was so knocked out because he had been asked to pose with Ros, in a boiler suit. He was really over the moon and came in very proudly one day and brandished this newspaper and said; "Have you seen this? Look, that's me and my old lady." He was absolutely enthralled because there was a picture of him and Ros in boiler suits. And I thought, "How sweet. He has so much talent and so much to offer. and yet he is going around all excited because someone asked him to do some fashion pictures."'

Rick did find the constant Press attentions, however, rather surprising. 'When you're used to being just a face in a crowd, it's unnerving when people keep phoning for interviews,' he confided in a friend.

As they toured the country, the *Strawbs* became not only known for their music, but also their astonishing consumption of alcohol. The group's recollections of those days are more than tinged with an alcoholic haze. Dave Cousins claims they were the biggest drinking group in the country.

'There was no one to touch us. At that time I was running a folk club in the *White Bear*, Hounslow, so Rick decided he'd like to have his own folk club at Acton, and he called it the Booze Droop. Sort of competition, I suppose. He was going to call it 'Brewers Droop.' (A printing error in the first advert in *Melody Maker* called the club, Booze Droop, and so Rick and his partner Colin Spiers decided to let it stick at that.)

'We had stupid things there like a drinking competition against the *Melody Maker*. Their team came down, and a team from the White Bear. We challenged and beat the lot very easily, because we could outdrink anybody at that time. We used to go completely out of our minds most of the time. That was the trouble. We got on so well that, as Rick has said, nobody dared tell anybody else they were wrong. We were such good mates. We spent all our time together.'

To start with, the Booze Droop, held in a large room at the Acton pub where *The Who* began their career, was a huge success. People like David Bowie and Big Jim Sullivan popped in to make guest appearances, at what Rick called his alcoholic arts lab. Because of contractual difficulties, Rick was not allowed to advertise his star attractions, but the crowds came just the same. However, on the nights the regulars knew Rick would not be able to make it, the numbers dropped dramatically.

The Strawbs were still not earning a lot of money despite their new-found fame. Wakeman remembers: 'To cut the bills, when we arrived at a hotel one trick was that the one who was smartest dressed would go and book the room nearest the fire escape. All the rest of us used to leap up the escape. I once slept in a room where a guy called Gordon, our Scottish roadie, was on the left-hand side of the bed, I was in the middle and Hud was on the right.'

Smiling still at the memory of those days, Cousins said: 'It was just drink, drink, drink - all the time. Rick used to come over to the *White Bear* on Sunday lunchtimes when it was a general musical knees-up. I had the folk club there on Sunday evenings. And Rick would get up on the stage and read pornographic poems that he used to write - and probably still does. He had those great long, blue Eskimo-Nell-type poems which he used to read. I used to take our publicist there, and we would get journalists down. They were astonished at these performances.'

With the help of his outside session work and his £30 a week from the *Strawbs*, Rick and Ros managed to move from their flat in Ilford to a terraced house in West Harrow, not far from Harrow School. The modest home was the first faltering step along the road to super success.

The *Harrow Observer* welcomed Wakeman to its circulation area with this strange headline:

'STRAWBS VIRTUOSO MOVES INTO HARROW. Rick Wakeman has been acclaimed tomorrow's superstar and pop find of 1970, but who is he?'

Beat Instrumental certainly knew who he was all right. It carried a page profile on Wakeman. The writer said: 'Rick has suddenly been latched on to by the Press as a new discovery sensation, but he's been playing since he was six, starting with piano lessons.'

The writer continued:

> While the *Strawbs* look as if they're really going to make it at last, Rick still has some solo things to be done. 'I'd love to do a solo L.P., but I haven't got the money even to get the people I want and make a demo. I've got it all written - a pop symphony, jazz suites, and other things - but none of it's been performed yet.'

> Some reviewers felt that Rick's career would shortly develop away from the *Strawbs*. But he knows a good thing when he's in it: 'We really are a ridiculously happy band, and we're getting through to people more and more. I think we've got a very good sound that's all our own, and I'm sure it'll happen for us.'

> One factor could be that the *Strawbs*, unlike many bands, tend to have friends rather than fans. 'Out on gigs you can always find us in the bar talking to people. I think that's good. We all love meeting the people who are supplying us with a living.'

But as the weeks went by and despite his comments, Rick began to get more and more disillusioned with the *Strawbs*. Gus Dudgeon takes up the story: 'Rick had taken time off from the group to play for Elton John's first Festival Hall concert, and I asked him there how he was getting on and he said he was pissed off, which I could believe because I had worked with the *Strawbs*, and once produced 'Strawbs', an early album which included the controversial 'Man Who Called Himself Jesus' track. Dave Cousins was, in my opinion, completely authoritarian and usually wouldn't let anybody do any of their own songs. Everything had to be a Dave Cousins song and everything had to be done his way. He was silly, because it was because of Dave that the *Strawbs* had so many personnel changes.

'There was another guy who was with the band who I thought was a very talented singer - a guy called Tony Hooper. He was in the original *Strawbs* and was a great singer and had written some good songs, but there was no way they were going to get played. And funnily enough Rick was realizing the fact that he was starting to write choral pieces and he felt there was no way the *Strawbs* were ever going to do them. This was possibly an indication that the days of Rick with the *Strawbs* were numbered.'

Rick says: 'I composed a lot of songs, but none of them were deemed suitable for *Strawbs*. We all used to write, but the *Strawbs* then was Dave Cousins and his music was so good to play. He was undoubtedly the *Strawbs* classical writer. When you heard the group you knew songs had the Cousins stamp on them. Lovely melodies with brilliant lyrics. One of the signs of the way things were going was when everybody started writing songs. I was then happy just arranging the music. Eventually complacency crept into the band, including myself. Everybody had moved up to £30 a week and could live quite happily on that. We used to have rehearsals and Dave and I would learn the music beforehand and work out the arrangements. We'd turn up at ten in the morning and the rest of the lads would straggle in whenever they felt like it.'

What did Cousins think of Rick's composing talents in those days? 'The music just wasn't in the context of the group,' he said. 'The lyrics were awful. And in the end I had to tell him so. He got so hurt and upset it was dreadful. But I thought that I just had to tell him. We tried hard, we tried to sing the lyrics, we tried to sing them straight, we tried to sing them seriously, we tried to sing them humorously. But no way did the lyrics work at all. I tried to rewrite them. We got somebody else to try to rewrite them - in case he got offended because it was a member of the group rewriting them. And all in all, those lyrics didn't work.

'Rick's songs, at that time, were dreadful. They just didn't make it. As a piano-player and interpreter, there was no one better. I still maintain that he is the best keyboard interpreter of anybody's songs that I have ever heard. He's really exceptionally fluid. But, at that time, his own personal creativity wasn't too hot. He was inventive melodically, but his lyrics were pretty grim. And I think even now he admits that his lyrics aren't as hot as they might be. But he's working hard at it. And I admire him for trying.'

Although Cousins was not Rick's biggest fan as a composer, the BBC recognized the Wakeman skill quickly. Rick wrote and played the theme music for the TV's *Ask Aspel* show, and it is still in use.

But Cousins could find nothing wrong with his playing skills. He said: 'Rick was far beyond my technique. But we somehow seemed to work together.'

He remembers a time when they were rehearsing a Cousins song called 'Sheep' in Cousins's front room in Hounslow, Middlesex.

'I said, "I think we ought to have an intro like this," and, quite by chance, I picked up the guitar and played a few notes all the way up the scale. Rick said, "Hang on. What did you do?" And I couldn't for the life of me remember what I had done. It was just pure fluke that I came out with all the right notes. He reproduced exactly what I had played and said, "That's a great introduction - we'll use that." So he would continually push me. Whatever I wanted him to play, he was capable of playing. There didn't seem to be anything he couldn't play.

'Rick would adapt the open-tunings of my songs and turn them into piano chords, and it would give a great melodic sound. It all worked well together and was very effective. He forced me into doing new things all the time. He was nothing short of a genius.'

I asked Dave Cousins if it was hard for him having written all the songs, to see someone else come in and almost take all the publicity?

'No,' he said, 'it was good for me, because Rick was still interpreting my songs, which was to my advantage. It was very much a group, although Rick was getting a lot of the publicity - the majority of the publicity. It was very much a group identity; nobody resented anything. There was no bad feeling. Despite the success, however, things were quickly starting to fall apart. And rumours came thick and fast in the music Press that Rick was about to leave the group for 'better things'. This naturally caused friction within the *Strawbs*. 'Rick's last date with us was in Norwich,' added Cousins. 'He had exaggerated his prowess throughout the evening in all matters. He had drunk more than anybody. We were getting fed up with this because it was obvious he was going to leave us anyway. He became unbearable. So we decided it was time he was put down a bit.

'He was in the van after the gig saying: "I feel sick and ill." It was snowing outside, so we stopped the van and he fell out in the snow. We left him there, in a Tee-shirt. Then we got a bit worried after about five minutes. It was a question of who held out the longest. And we thought he probably was ill. So we got him back in the van and started to say in loud whispers, "Let's take him to the hospital", thinking he'd come round and say he was all right. But either he was ill, or he had the courage to keep going. So we took him to hospital. He was carried in over the shoulder of our roadie, who dumped him with a nurse. Half an hour later, he was wheeled out slumped in a wheelchair. They said there was nothing wrong with him that a stomach pump and a good night's sleep wouldn't cure.'

Cousins says that Rick's biggest weakness at that time was his habit of exaggerating. 'It was always a standing joke that if you divided everything he claimed by two, you were near to the right figure. If he said he had drunk sixteen pints of beer, he had probably drunk eight. Anyway, we got to making the second album with him, which was 'From the Witchwood'. We started off very well. It was very encouraging. The first track we put down was 'The Hangman and the Papist'. That was recorded "live" in the studio. But then Rick seemed to be off doing sessions all the time and things started to go wrong. There would be four of us in there putting down the tracks - and Rick's part was always being dubbed on. Some of the songs he and I saw totally eye-to-eye on. He loved 'A Glimpse of Heaven' and 'A

Shepherd's Song '. He couldn't stand 'Thirty Days' and some other songs like 'Flight'. Those were the songs which the pair of us didn't like. He liked the others and really got on well with them. He was disappointed with his solo on 'Sheep' which he thought he could have done much better; and he wrote a song himself, which had so many chord changes that nobody could keep up with it.'

There were certainly many problems in putting 'From the Witchwood' together. There were endless rows in the group about what should be used on the album. This trouble over ironing out material led to the band paying out a fortune in recording three times as much material as needed for 'Witchwood', and in the last-minute withdrawal of a plan to release a single from the album. No one in the band could agree which track should be released as a forty-five.

Regular hints kept appearing in the music Press about the possibility of Rick leaving.

One journalist reported: 'I knew there was tension in the band - who doesn't have disagreements? - but the extent soon became apparent to me.'

Rick told Mark Plummer of *Melody Maker*, who in those early days did more than any other rock journalist to further Rick's career, but later hurt him deeply by launching into a slashing attack on 'Six Wives': 'Now we are coming to the crunch where the band have come to realize that I hate folk music - I loathe it. I like the people playing and I can see their reasons for doing so, but all the same I just loathe it. We've moved on from the days of the Strawberry Hill boys, the days when an audience of forty in a pub was good. We're a rock band. And rock isn't just Deep Purple with volume, rock is something musically clever and entertaining and half of the rock music I hear is diabolical.

'Kids now want to hear something musically clever, not just two or three chords churned out, and half the bands doing that just treat their audience as _____ . The funny thing is that half of those kids know more about music than the people on stage playing it. Kids might not understand how to read music, but they understand something that is theirs.'

Dave Cousins says the gradual split still left them the best of friends. 'There were never blows. We all got hurt with one another; but never blows because we were not that sort of group. We spent all our available time together. Wives and girlfriends were completely forgotten if we were in the pub together. And that included any member of the band with anybody else, Rick included. If we were in the pub with anybody then that was it. We played darts together. We had a darts team - the best darts team. And we were the best drinking team. It was just comradeship all the way down the line.'

Dave affirms that success in the commercial music world had no effect on him or the group in those heady days. 'I mean it's the trendy image not to drink beer. But we all would go down the boozer, drink beer, and get drunk. I couldn't mope around all the time looking long-faced, or stoned out of my mind and serious. That's not us and never will be. We just enjoy ourselves.'

He told a reporter: 'The strain of wondering what to do was taking its toll on Rick's health.'

Chas Cronk told me: 'Shortly after he had got the house in Harrow I went across with my wife to see Rick and Ros. He was looking really strained at that time because he was working with the *Strawbs* and still doing sessions. He would finish a gig and then go straight into the studio until the early hours of the morning. I remember thinking then that he looked really ill, but Rick would never have that. Rick is one of those that would work until the death. I don't think he really considers his health too much. I think his attitude was always: "If I go, I go with a bang."'

But then a middle-of-the-night phone call was to change the course of Rick Wakeman's career.

He recalled: 'I had been doing a lot of sessions and was lying in bed after having done a three-day stint with about six hours of sleep. And that was typical. I had just arrived home having had no sleep again, and fell into bed. It was one of those things where the minute my head hit the pillow, I fell asleep. It felt so good, and then the phone rang. I couldn't believe it. I covered my earholes up and Ros picked up the phone. I could hear the conversation. "He's only just come in. He hasn't been back for three days – you know he's really tired."

I was awake by then and let me tell you I was furious. "Gimme that phone . . . who's that?" I said. And this voice said, "Oh, hello. It's Chris Squire from *Yes*." (See above) It's three in the morning mind you, and he said, "How . . . how are you?" I said, "You phone me up at three in the morning to ask how I am?" I told him I was very tired and asked him if he would phone back. "Well," he said, "We've just come back from an American tour and we're thinking of having a change in personnel. I saw you doing some sessions down at Advision Studios and all I wanted to know was if you'd be interested in joining the band." And I like a berk said, "No!" and slammed the phone down. I was furious.

'I woke up the next morning and said, "Who the hell was that on the phone?" Ros told me what had happened. So, I raked through my record collection and pulled out *Yes*'s 'Time and a Word'. I hadn't really got into it that much and I had hardly played it. So I played it and thought, "Yeah, this is interesting. Maybe I shouldn't have said no . . . to *Yes* after all.'"

SEVEN

The Acceptable Face of Rock-Biz

A furtive meeting in a tiny London pub was to clinch Rick Wakeman's decision to say yes to *Yes*, and become the anchor man of what is probably the most musically brilliant rock group in the world. The ale house in Shepherd's Market was the venue for the clandestine meeting with the group at the request of Brian Lane, *Yes's* ambitious manager.

Lane, the moustachioed financial genius who started his rock career as manager of girl singer Anita Harris, had become involved with *Yes*, now acknowledged leaders of 'intellectual pop', during a period in the early seventies when he ran a highly unsuccessful London record production company called Mum and Dad Music. 'I was then trying to produce an English version of Tamla Motown,' said Lane. 'Although we were called Mum and Dad Music, all we could produce was little bastards. I didn't have one hit. I started to manage *Yes* when I needed a rock'n'roll band for these terrible records. *Yes* fitted the bill in those days. But they soon started to do really well, then they decided they wanted to replace their keyboard player, Tony Kaye.

I had used Rick on about thirty of my doomed Tamla Motown sessions. He had been recommended to me by fixer David Katz. We didn't exactly get off to a good start, though, because the first I saw of him in the studio was his back. I shouted: "No women in the studio." With a sweep of his long blond hair, he turned round and retorted, "How dare you." But he was very good, though I could see he hated what he was doing. He knew English-style Tamla Motown wasn't going to make it. Anyway, we became sort of friends. I owed him money for the sessions, so we kept in contact.

'When the group said they wanted to replace Tony Kaye, I immediately recommended Rick, but they were doubtful because he was still playing with the *Strawbs*. Anyway, I phoned Rick and said, "Do you want to join *Yes*?" and he said bluntly, "NO." So I asked him why, and he explained his position with the *Strawbs*. I then offered him £5 a week more than he was getting with the *Strawbs*, and Rick, being a man of very strong principles and loyalty, said, "I accept."'

That was a slightly exaggerated version of the story. Actually Rick didn't accept straightaway and he arranged the meeting with Lane and the band in the pub. As he walked in, the group, as a man, gasped,

'Oh my God, is this supposed to be the new keyboards genius?' Then one of them added, 'He's a bit big isn't he?' And as the conspirators chatted amid the smoke and foamy pints, Rick threw them all with a rather strange request. 'If I join the band I'd like to bring my paint rollers,' he said firmly.

Commented a tongue-in-cheek Lane: 'I didn't really know what he meant by that. I thought he wanted to be in charge of decorating the band's bus or something! It later transpired that Rick used to like walking up and down the keyboards with his paint rollers. I've heard of people like this. You read about them every Sunday in the *News of the World*. So I thought I had better humour him and go along with his paint rollers, though I thought, "The first sign of a tin of Dulux, and I'll elbow him."'

But, all humour aside, it was not just paint rollers that Rick was interested in. He pointedly asked Jon Anderson (pictured above): 'How much do you earn a week?' Jon told him and Rick, in return, told him of the £35 a week he had been picking up with the *Strawbs*. Anderson's reaction was: 'Well our offer's a sight more than you're getting and everything we've got, we own.'

Rick's next question was: 'What plans have you got?' Anderson said they were going to America and Rick surprised all of them by saying he didn't want to go. He left the pub having said 'No' to the possibility of becoming a member of one of the world's most brilliant groups – for what? Apparently, life with the *Strawbs* and the chance of more gruelling sessions.

'Anyway, I went home and thought "I must be mad",' said Rick. "I mean, someone had offered me a really good job with a band I really admired, and I was holding out. I thought, "What a berk" and went

back and joined immediately.'

The new *Yes* man soon became the world's first keyboards player to surround himself with an amphitheatre of instruments - something that at first really appealed to the group. They had just had their first big hit L.P., 'The Yes Album', and Wakeman added a glamorous new dimension to the band. *Melody Maker* devoted the whole of their front page to the news of the 'NEW YES MAN'.

The article read:

> Rick Wakeman has joined *Yes* after the shock departure of organist Tony Kaye. *Yes*'s shock news came after a week of rumours and has surprised fans of both groups - although the *M.M.* reported earlier this year that there was a likelihood of Wakeman quitting the *Strawbs*.
>
> It is the second big change for *Yes*: lead guitarist Peter Banks left last year and was replaced by Steve Howe (above).
>
> Wakeman (21) has already started work recording with *Yes* on their next album

'Fragile'. He will debut with them at the start of their British tour.

This will be on 30th September (1971) at the de Montfort Hall, Leicester. Rick will be playing organ, piano, Mellotron, Moog synthesizer, and electric keyboards, and will also write for future albums.

Part of the reason for the split was that Tony Kaye wanted to concentrate on Hammond Organ while *Yes* wanted to further augment their sound. And said Tony: 'I'd not been happy with the band for a year really, and wasn't getting into the new music they were playing. It was difficult to get my ideas across, and in the States we were drifting apart socially.'

Wakeman commented: 'The truth is that I found that I could offer more to *Yes* musically and they could offer me more because I found that I had reached my peak within the *Strawbs*. I think the *Strawbs* had got as far as they could with the present line-up, and the change will help them to move in a new direction.'

How right Rick was. Although this switch looked like being a disaster for the *Strawbs*, Brian Lane points out that they never had a hit record while Rick was with them. 'They only started to happen when he left,' he said. For soon the *Strawbs* were in the singles charts with hits like 'Part of the Union', which had them regularly appearing on *Top of the Pops*. However, the group split further when Hud and John Ford decided to form a duo and had great success as *Hudson Ford*.

Cousins is now the only member of that vintage *Strawbs* group left in the band who are still relatively successful, but have never recaptured those heady days with Rick and their later teenybopper success.

Before Wakeman actually legally joined *Yes*, a lot of delicate negotiating had to be done between record companies and managements. Explained Derek Green, present British head of A&M Records and then boss of Rondor Music, *Yes*'s publishers: 'The situation was that Rick was signed to A&M Records as one of the *Strawbs*, but also as an individual. So when the company heard that Rick was joining *Yes* we wanted a word with their record company, Atlantic. A&M decided to give the right for Rick to record for them with *Yes* in return for having him for solo albums.

'It was obviously an interesting situation because up until then Rick had not made a solo album, but A&M believed in him, knowing his great technique. When it came to negotiating the contracts, A&M had an American attorney come over to represent them. We got into one of those crazy negotiations that can go on forever, or so it seems. The manager of the *Strawbs* was there, as was Brian Lane who represented *Yes* and Rick. I was there also.

'So it was one of those amazingly long-drawn-out negotiations where eventually everyone thought they had won. Probably they had. I think that, actually, everything that Rick does works out in a way that everybody wins. So at the end of these talks everybody had forgotten the real point of the arguments, and that was a Rick Wakeman solo album. After it was all sewn up, our American attorney said to me: "How does Rick sing?" I just broke up and said, "I don't think he does." "He doesn't sing. Does he write?" "I don't know." This was just gorgeous. That's how silly rock'n'roll can get.'

The news of Rick's move to *Yes* had accidentally reached A&M at an open-air concert at London's Crystal Palace where *Yes* were the main attraction. 'I happened to be there for a summer concert by the group and Brian Lane was there also,' said Green. 'One of the people I had taken with me was Larry Yaskiel, then British and European head of A&M Records. I wanted to introduce this guy to Brian and when we met, he took us into *Yes*'s back-stage caravan.

Brian didn't know who Larry was and he confided: 'You won't believe what's happening to *Yes*. We're stealing Rick Wakeman from the *Strawbs*.' Larry's face was an absolute picture. I said, 'Brian, I think before you go any further, I must introduce you to Larry Yaskiel, who's the head of A&M Records in England.'

The day Rick joined *Yes* wasn't quite 'the day the earth stood still', but it did cause an upheaval and a tremor which resounded throughout rock. Tony Kaye's departure and the intake of Rick, was a traumatic episode which upset not a few admirers of the band, especially because of the apparently ruthless way in which it was done.

With the success of their third L.P., 'The Yes Album', which by then had sold 60,000 copies in the U.K, alone, and with exciting prospects in America, it was time for *Yes* to stop and take a look at the future. They wanted to introduce new material, new sounds, and expand the *Yes* style. Their ideas didn't fit in with Tony Kaye's. Kaye said: 'I like to go out and meet people when we have finished a gig. The others liked to go back to their hotel rooms. And the three guitarists - Steve, Chris and Jon - would be working out new numbers, which was difficult for me, only able to play organ on stage. So the rest were getting it together and I wasn't part of it.

'All this started quite a long time ago. When we first got the new band together, it was happy and creative. But later, we weren't writing, or in the studios, just doing concerts, and there was not time for me to practise. I quite dig what was put down on the last L.P. but I'm not very happy with the stuff I played. The way I feel at the moment, I want to rest from being on the road and business scenes. I just want time to think. I've been on the road and playing for six years. I feel disappointed at leaving as a founder member. It's a good band, playing its own music. But now I want to do something different. I think the split will do us both a lot of good. Anyone can change, and it's happened to us. They wanted me to play Moog and Mellotron and other keyboards, but I just wanted to play organ.'

Yes lead vocalist Jon Anderson said: 'The split was a bit strange and a freaky thing. Tony is a tremendous guy and in the years we were together he was very efficient and great for the band. Getting Steve in changed us and visiting the States gave us greater realization of the potential. We wanted a more colourful sound and Tony was content to groove along, which was nice. But we know how good Rick was, and he has proved tremendous. It's so exciting to work with somebody like him. I think he's been bottled up in the past and now it's all pouring out. It was very hard to make the change, but we shall be friends with Tony.

'There is something about Rick that turned me on completely. He's very enthusiastic and very talented and already it feels as if he has been in the band for years. Him and Steve get on very well. The band will always carry on, and if one person lags, then there's got to be a change. It's very strange that the next L.P. title is 'Fragile'! We just want to create the best music we can.'

As an album, the record was far from fragile. In fact, Rick still feels it was the best the band made while he was with them for the first period. It was put together at Advision's sixteen-track studio in London. Engineer for the classic album was Eddie Offord, a small, pinched-faced man who has guided the fortunes of *Emerson, Lake and Palmer*, among others.

Rick described the way *Yes* were moving into orchestral rock. 'You've had the heavy bands such as *Cream* and *The Who*, now we are trying to move on one stage further into orchestral rock,' he said. 'I think we have the same excitement that heavy rock generated, but what *Yes* are doing is a hell of a lot more complicated and musically refined. Every bar is thought out when the song is formulated. Once the whole thing is together you can play it as you feel it, but there is a solid backbone and arrangement to work from. We're working eighteen hours a day recording and rehearsing, and some of the things that are coming out are just - well, they're silly.' Silly? 'You know Steve [Howe] will get a really fast riff and instead of just the guitar taking it we're putting it out together. When we finish we just have to laugh, it seems frighteningly impossible. I don't really know how to explain it.

'The way *Yes* think is amazing too, Bill is not just a drummer and Chris is not just a bass player - can you follow that? Jon doesn't just think like a singer either, they all think like the true musicians they are. Suggest a straight and obvious bass line to Chris, and you might as well forget about it before you start.'

Shortly after joining the band he revealed in a *Sounds* interview with Penny Valentine how difficult it had been to fit in with *Yes*. Rick said: 'It's not been an easy band to just slide into because we don't really mix socially - which is good really because I don't think music and social life mix very well. I mean we all argue after gigs anyway. The first time I met them I couldn't believe a group could argue so much. I thought they were about to split up and thought "Oh well, there's £100 and a job out of the window." But then I found they just argue, everyone tells everyone else when they think they've played badly on a gig. They're all total individuals.'

Rick then revealed a secret - that he had planned to form his own band with a bassist, guitarist and drummer before the *Yes* offer came along. They even did music for a Liz Taylor-Michael Caine film *Zee and Co.* He did part of the musical score while still with the *Strawbs*. Rick explained: 'I had done some session work for Stanley Myers - he's the guy who arranged the music for the film *Percy* - and he asked me if I'd like to write eighteen minutes of rock music for a film that was being released. It was all over in ten days. There were two numbers - 'Coat of Many Colours' and 'Whirlwind'.'

Then 'Fragile' was released on 1st November 1971. It included 'Heart of the Sunrise', plus three other group tracks, 'Roundabout', 'South Side of the Sky', 'Long Distance Runaround', and five short individual tracks - one from each member of the band - Rick's 'Cans and Brahms', Jon Anderson's 'We Have Heaven', Bill Bruford's 'Five Per Cent for Nothing', Chris Squire's 'The Fish', and Steve Howe's 'Mood for a Day'. Rick, for 'Cans and Brahms', took extracts from the third movement of Brahms's Fourth Symphony in E minor and played different instrument parts on different keyboards. He put down six electric piano tracks, four organ parts, two on harpsichord and one on Moog.

When 'Fragile' was completed the band had agreed on a sleeve by top designer Roger Dean. Each member had a section to himself. Rick decided he wanted to include some pictures of himself at Brentford Football Club's Griffin Park ground, in West London. Since his childhood, Wakeman, now a Vice-President, has been a fanatical supporter of the club and still attends all the games he can. So he phoned them up and asked if the pictures could be taken. He was given a curt refusal, which hurt him deeply.

The L.P. quickly shot to the top of both the British and American album charts - and Brentford F.C. missed the chance of worldwide fame.

Dennis Piggot, Brentford general manager, now a good friend of Rick's, told me guardedly after the record had been awarded its first gold disc for $1 million sales in America. 'If he wishes for pictures to be taken in the future, we would be happy to talk to him about it.'

As the album went into the British charts, *Yes* began on a countrywide tour, and soon the Press recorded that they had moved from a 'good group' to a 'super-group'. All since Wakeman had joined them.

Ray Coleman wrote about their Festival Hall appearance in *Melody Maker*:

> There are groups with outstanding soloists who dominate; there are groups without solo stars, and here the aim is usually to merge all the talents so that no one stands out. Both policies can be successful. But rarely has a group gathered so much cohesion as *Yes*, and few groups can boast such a winning mixture of dazzling soloists and total togetherness. The precision and tightness of their performance at London's Royal Festival Hall on Friday, was staggering. Two encores insisted on their return to the stage. At the end of the night, *Yes* had been elevated to superstar status.
>
> They proved they deserve most of the superlatives that have been heaped on them. Five musicians, beautifully complementing each other, blend into a joyful sound which, while keeping its roots firmly in rock, strives successfully for a non-raucous gloss. None of the players is incapable of fierce, aggressive and exciting solo work - but the *Yes* sound excites more after its shiny sparkle.

And as the praise poured in, so did the cash. Soon after joining *Yes*, Rick began to benefit from the amazing financial wizardry of Brian Lane, of the gimlet-like blue eyes. For instance, in 1973 *Yes* grossed in excess of seven figures, half of it earned in America. After all expenses had been accounted for, the members of the group received between fifty and sixty per cent of the net, making them one of the world's highest-paid bands.

And by adopting a perfectly legal policy favoured by most public celebrities, *Yes* signed away their overseas earnings into trust for the sake of taxation benefits.

Brian Lane, who once flunked his accountancy finals, insisted that once a manager has helped a band to attain a successful footing, it's his duty to advise them on any financial transactions in which they may wish to involve themselves. His guidance has given them the chance of lifetime security. And for his invaluable services, Lane received one-sixth of the *Yes* income, out of which he settled all his own expenses including all travel.

On his advice, *Yes* placed their earnings in the hands of an accountant. As it is not easy for musicians to get mortgages, Lane helped them with property investments as mortgage interests are tax deductible.

He explained to Roy Carr in *New Musical Express*: 'I've made *Yes* invest by quoting this maxim: "Invest in land because they've stopped making it. Don't invest in show business because they'll never stop making it." I always tell the boys to put their money in something tangible. For instance, I got them all to buy Rolls-Royces. Not new ones but models you can buy which will appreciate in value. They've also found out it's cheaper to buy antique furniture than the new stuff you find in the High Street, and where possible we deal direct with the manufacturers when purchasing new equipment. *Yes* have become the original discount kids. Now this may sound like we're a real bunch of mercenaries, but you must realize that even if a group are lucky, they may enjoy a five – six-year run. However, you must never cut corners at the expense of the people who put you there, and by that I mean the public.'

One of Lane's first pieces of advice to Rick when he joined the group – he started at £50 a week but within a short time the band were grossing so much on records and concerts that they went on percentages - was to buy a large house.

'Ros and I were very happy living in our little terraced house in West Harrow, but Brian insisted that it would be a good investment to buy a larger house,' said Rick.

'So I took a drive over to Gerrards Cross in Buckinghamshire, a stockbroker-and-pink-gin area, and went into the poshest estate agents I could find. I had seen a house called 'Southgate' in the window for sale at £26,500 and so I told the chap, "I'd like that one." I am sure he thought I was mad, especially as I was dressed more like a tramp than a rich young man.

'Anyway, he arranged for me to see round it and although Ros and I had doubts about the area, we decided to go ahead. We never really felt at ease the whole time we were there. One night I decided to try and be friendly with the locals and so I went into the pub and got chatting to one of them. Looking at my appearance he said, "Passing through?" I said, "No, I've just bought 'Southgate'.' His face dropped and I could feel he was disgusted that "hippy types" could be allowed into such an area.

'When I finally did sell up and move to Farnham Common I made a point of going into the pub and telling this particular gentleman that I had sold "Southgate" to a man called Mr Patel. That was the final straw for him!'

Besides investing in property, Rick was advised to put his money into classical cars. And he was given a great start by Gerry Moss, the 'M' in A&M Records. He presented Rick with a 22-foot 1957 Cadillac which was once used in a film by Clark Gable. Rick had it shipped over from the States, installed a television, and quadraphonic sound, and even put an Axminster carpet in it.

'I was offered £14,000 for it recently, but I am not selling,' he told me one day, adjusting his £2,000 gold wrist-watch like someone who has just won the pools. Big is no exaggeration. This monster on wheels - it takes up two parking meters - has a thirty-gallon petrol tank, and on a good run does seven miles to the gallon.

'When I first had it I was only getting three miles to the gallon,' said Rick. 'But my mechanic did a marvellous job to make it more economical.'

Gradually Rick built up his collection to twenty cars, including eight Rolls-Royces, two Bentleys, two Jaguars, plus the super-luxury Cadillac.

He even presented his mum and dad with a 1958 Silver Cloud and gave Ros a £4,000 XJ6 Jaguar for Christmas. I suppose you could argue that I didn't need all those beautiful Rolls-Royces,' he said. 'But I happen to enjoy driving them. I am also a great believer in buying things that appreciate in value. And of course, cars like this do.'

As Rick's business acumen grew with experience, he decided not to let the cars just rot, but put them to good use. So he set up the Fragile Carriage Company in Twickenham and rented out the cars he wasn't using at the time for weddings, films and big occasions.

Rick took on a full-time mechanic to look after the moving parts of the £85,000 worth of cars, and also a Rolls-Royce trained trimmer to keep their insides in immaculate order.

As a *Yes*-man he was well and truly part of the acceptable face of rock-biz.

EIGHT

'I'll Have Brentford F.C. for £1 Million, Please'

I hear we're playing the next gig in My-Rand,' said the caped crusader, leaning heavily on the bar of a Paris hotel.

'My-Rand?' said Chris Squire innocently and looking somewhat puzzled.

'Your round? Good, then I'll have a whisky sour,' pounced the triumphant Wakeman. 'And a lager chaser.'

'You've had one bloody drink already,' grumbled Squire, who was crestfallen at Wakeman's one-upmanship. He reluctantly paid up and left the grinning blond giant at the bar.

Tricks like that hardly endeared Rick to the more serious members of the band. But his practical joking certainly did not interfere with his or their on-stage performances. Like their later night of triumph at the Palais des Sports, or when they took Madison Square Garden, New York, by storm in February 1974.

You could smell the sulphur in the air that heady night as thousands of fans lit matches to show their appreciation of *Yes*, and their brilliant keyboards king, Rick Wakeman. It was America's way of saying 'yes' to the super-group, and Rick in particular. Lighting matches and turning down the lights had become a common sight at U.S. concerts, but it was doubtful whether the Garden had seen quite so many brilliant spots of light after a concert as it did when *Yes* played a couple of sell-out shows, with 20,000 fans at each concert.

Wakeman's cascading finger-work took the breath away as they tried to comprehend how anyone could play in such a way. His long pointed fingers whirled from Moog to Mellotron to piano to organ as his shimmering cape trailed around the mountain of keyboards.

'We played well tonight,' said the 6-foot 4-inch Wakeman later as he stepped from the dressing-room shower, towelling his ox frame. 'It was the kind of show I wish we could play every night – the best *Yes* concert I've ever experienced.'

The Garden shows opened with three tracks from their 'Close to the Edge' album: 'Siberian Khatru', 'And You and I' and the title track, all of which were greeted warmly by audiences obviously well familiar with these pieces. It was obvious this would be a night to cherish. But this was the aperitif, with the main course yet to come.

The highlight - and test - of the show was putting their new work - all four sides of 'Tales From Topographic Oceans', an awful lot of music to present to an audience first-time round.

Guitarist Steve Howe and Wakeman came away with honours. Howe for his brilliantly sustained guitar work, using all manner of different instruments, and Wakeman for his underlying presence throughout the entire piece.

'Wakeman is a keyboard king of the highest order. Without him *Yes* would lose all the power of the show,' Chris Charlesworth wrote in *Melody Maker*. 'Rick Wakeman's choice of keyboards is legendary, and the effects at his fingertips are many and varied.'

It wasn't just his keyboard work that grabbed the attention, but also his shimmering cape, which by now had become the hallmark of all his stage appearances. So how did the cape become part of the Wakeman stage finery? The person who makes them all is an elegant leggy blonde called Denise Gandrup from Cleveland, Ohio, who became Cape Maker by Appointment for Rick Wakeman by accident.

It all began at Kent State University, Ohio, scene of the dreadful campus shooting where four students were killed by the National Guard. Denise was planning to attend a *Yes* concert there, and was looking round first with a friend, who was then going out with the group's lighting man, Michael Tait.

'I was at design college and had made myself a black velvet cape,' said Denise, who is of Norwegian extraction. 'I had left the cape in an empty dressing-room and gone looking round the place. Thinking the room was still empty I went back to collect the cape, but to my horror I found the group were in there changing. It was very embarrassing, especially as Michael had told me, "Never go near them, they're ogres!" Karen and I were scared to death and I just wanted to run.

'As I tried to get out of the room, Rick called, "Wait a minute." He wanted to know more about my cape. Before I knew it Karen began telling him how I had also made a sequined jacket. I was then surrounded by Brian Lane, Jon Anderson, Rick, and just about everyone else in there. They said they were doing a gig at the Rainbow in London and asked if I could make a sequined cloak for Rick. I agreed and did it in silver and sent it to him with a bill for 200 dollars. It took about two weeks of my spare time to complete. Rick was so pleased that he sent me a telegram saying he would pay 300 dollars.

'The cape was really good for their lighting because it reflected all the colours. It is probably the cape that people remember most.'

Rick had been looking for something to wear on stage for a long time. Most clothes restricted his speedy switches from keyboard to keyboard, but the cape was the ideal answer. It proved to be the first in a long, glittering line.

The second Wakeman cape was completed in England, after Denise graduated from college. 'I flew to England but couldn't get a work permit to do a regular job, so Rick came along and asked me if I would do a cape for the 'Topographic Oceans' tour. That one was gold with sequins all over it. It also had orange and red colours on its side. It was a kaftan-type and that was the last of that type I did because Rick found all that weight on his arms was not good for playing, said Denise. 'It was rather beautiful, though, with hundreds of thousands of sequins on it.'

Rick with legendary DJ Alan "Fluff" Freeman (1927-2006)

The most ambitious cape of the five Denise has made for Rick was the one that she created for the Wembley ice show of 'King Arthur'. She recalled: 'We had twelve embroiderers working on it, a girl who did a chainmail top, plus the dyers. That cape cost more than £1,000 to do.'

Denise's cape for the 'No Earthly Connection' British and European tour with the English Rock Ensemble was meant to include fairylights, but Rick decided against them at the last moment.

'I really didn't want to risk being electrocuted on stage,' he explained.

Denise talked over the design of each new cape with him. 'Rick starts by asking me what I think, and when I have talked it over, he says, "Oh well, we'll do it this way." He just likes to see what you are going to say. Then I do the pattern. I get paid in three stages. One is the advance, one for the middle of the work and then a final payment when the cape is completed.'

But back to the music. 'Close to the Edge' was the second album that Wakeman played on with *Yes*. It was cut in 1972 at London's Advision Studios. At the time, the band announced that they had added a new 'member' - sound engineer, Eddie Offord. It was decided that Offord would tour with the band, and give them the kind of polished sound on stage that is such a characteristic of their albums.

Jon Anderson told Tony Stewart of the *New Musical Express* that the band had now reached what was almost total understanding in their music. In fact they were 'Close to the Edge'.

Anderson said: 'This is the whole point of the Album. 'Fragile' was the situation of the band at the time. The whole thing was like balancing on square corks on the swimming pool. The whole idea of the band at the time was very fragile, it could collapse. And as it happened it's taken off, and got better and better. Now we're close to the edge of spiritual awareness within the framework of the group, making music. It could depict crumbling into dust, or it could just carry on getting better and better. And we're not thinking about anything else than getting better and better. We're close to the edge of making music that might stand up in a few years' time.'

Stewart said that the recording of the new material - which is laid out as three lengthy tracks - received much careful consideration before they started recording.

Said Anderson: 'We have this long song, which we felt could hold a listener's ear for the whole length, rather than just a track here and there that they like. They can listen to it all, and that way they can get as much satisfaction as we get out of it. And we get a lot.

'Long pieces are something I've always wanted to do. Here it just seemed to happen. We never felt we had to make small tracks here, and small tracks there, for plays on the stations. We were just going to make the music, and hope that people will play it anyway if it's interesting enough.'

Anderson said that the song ideas are interrelated, and the feel of spiritual guidance - which is how he described it - is illustrated by the theme of 'Close to the Edge'.

Yet, when following the lyrics, many listeners could maybe not find it quite so easy to work out such enlightening statements, as Anderson describes his lyrical writing style as 'abstract'. It is this lyrical ambiguity and the possibilities of individual interpretations that give *Yes* music deeper interest.

'A lot of my words get abstract because I can't concentrate on one story line,' he said. 'The 'Siberian Khatru' track is just a lot of interesting sounding words, though it does relate to the dreams of clear

summer days. The title means winter, but it is meant to be the opposite. It doesn't really mean a great deal, but it's a nice tune, and that carries it.

'The other track, 'And You and I', could be classed as a hymn. Not in the sense of a church kind of thing. It's about feeling very, very secure in the knowledge of knowing there is somebody . . . God maybe.

'It's all working. We've worked at it two months now, and rehearsed every day. Then we spent the last month in the studio.'

Anderson then explained how the *Yes* musical co-operative worked. 'We sit down and bring individual ideas and we fix them together, like a jigsaw puzzle. It sounds like *Yes* music. That's the way we've always done it. We always bring in ideas from each other and kind of mix them all up and throw them on the floor, look at them, pick them up in the right parts, and put them together.'

He added: 'The music on 'Close to the Edge' is better than 'Fragile', at least to us. This one seems to be exactly where we wanted to be. It's taken a while to develop, but it's the right theme, the right title. Musically, we hope it'll be some heavy thing.'

To many *Yes* freaks, the sheer implication of the music is part of the attraction. But for a member of the band to admit he did not really understand it, came as quite a surprise. When 'Close to the Edge' was released, Rick admitted: 'It takes a hell of a lot of time to understand this album fully. In fact, it took me a long time to understand! I played a previous *Yes* record to some friends who really like the band, and they listened carefully and gave constructive criticisms. After I played 'Close to the Edge' they asked me to play it again and again – about four times - because they couldn't take it all in in one go.

'Basically the songs are very simple and the arrangements are complex. I like Jon's lyrics; they do make you think and derive your own meaning from them. I couldn't understand 'Heart of the Sunrise' (from 'Fragile'), originally, but I derived my own meaning from it. There's no "I love you baby, come to bed, let's do a 69 and dig my knees," about *Yes*.'

As they do with all their albums, *Yes* took the music on tour, playing it in full to packed houses across Europe and America. London's Rainbow Theatre was the setting for their biggest audience, for BBC's *Old Grey Whistle Test* televised the show.

The show, one of five at the Finsbury Park theatre in North London, was a big success, as Karl Dallas reported in *Melody Maker*. He said:

> There was one moment at London's Rainbow Theatre on Friday, during the glittering prelude to 'Close to the Edge', when the audience burst into spontaneous applause not at any particularly brilliant musical feat but at an exceptional theatrical effect.
>
> A glittering mirror ball like a giant-sized version of the ones you see in ballroom ceilings in big band films of the Glenn Miller era, during the smoochy music, came down at the back of the stage to be lit by powerful spotlights, filling the entire auditorium with circling fragments of light which were the exact visual counterpart of the sounds we were hearing.
>
> A simple thing like the fact that their 7,000 watts of PA is stereo, compared with

the mono systems most bands carry around with them, contributes so much to one's overall enjoyment of what they are doing.

Again, this isn't merely a question of re-creating the perfection of the recorded sound. There was one moment, during a Rick Wakeman Moog solo, when the sounds seemed to be leaping around directly above my head.

There are some who would argue that *Yes* are producing classical music for our time, and of course they make much of their classical roots, playing Stravinsky's Firebird Suite over the PA before they come on, and Jon Anderson humming the oboe solo from the beginning of Stravinsky's Rite of Spring, in a brief and almost unnoticed solo spot, but it is significant that they seem to have little contact with any classical music later than Schoenberg.

With the possible exception of Lenny Bernstein, classical music hasn't got room for extroverts these days, it's all got so solemn. It's a gap which was waiting for someone to fill, and *Yes* have done it brilliantly.

So perhaps in a sense, and in that sense alone, they are producing contemporary classics after all.

With so much Press attention, it was hardly surprising that more and more rock fans began to sit up and take notice of Wakeman. And the pop-paper readers' polls began to reflect the fact that here was a world-class musician playing with a world-class band.

In the 1972 *Melody Maker* poll, Wakeman was voted the world's number two keyboards man, just behind Keith Emerson. From 1973 onwards he has been voted the world's number one keyboards man each year in the *M.M.* poll, as he has in most of the other British pop papers. To topple Keith Emerson was no mean feat, but to continue to beat off the opposition for all these years certainly shows the calibre of the man.

Shortly after Wakeman joined *Yes*, they too began bringing in the awards, the first being in the 1973 *M.M.* poll when they were voted top band in both Britain and the world. Since then in most British papers they have been either top or around the top, in both sections.

Rick, after receiving his personal award and also the two for the band at the 1973 *M.M.* awards' party, said in typical fashion: 'I'd like to thank Watney Mann and Alka Seltzer who have helped my career.' Then he posed for photographers with a pint of Watney's beer perched on top of his award.

The band by now had become known as the 'Yes Electronic Circus' because of the size of their entourage. They were using three articulated lorries to carry their equipment and two mini-buses and a car. There were no less than nineteen roadies, which included three lighting and special-effects men, three more to operate the sound equipment, plus truck drivers and instrument men.

While the rest of the group travelled in style, these hard-working roadies had to load and unload twenty tons of equipment (including sixteen miles of cable) and often drove through the night to the next venue. All morning they would hump the equipment about, overcome crises in the lighting department, and arrange everything on stage according to the band's instructions.

Each member of the group also had his personal roadie, who took care of any personal problems. And Rick's had to take care of his keyboards.

Rick's personal collection of instruments was by now attracting much Press interest. 'I really believe I was one of the pioneers with keyboards, because it was unheard of to take a lot of them about on tour. The trouble was we didn't know how to amplify them because nobody had done it before,' said Rick. 'We just had to find out by trial and error and unfortunately that trial and error often took place on stage as well as off. Things were blowing up all the time and not working. I was determined to stick at it though, and I'm glad I did because there's hardly a guy in a pub these days who hasn't got at least three keyboards around him when he plays.

'The Press began taking my side and asking why manufacturers were not making the sort of equipment I needed. Since then the quality of keyboard instruments has just shot up.'

Derek Jewell, writing in the *SundayTimes*, said:

> Rick Wakeman, musician with *Yes*, sits in a studio recording the group's fifth album. Seven keyboard instruments surround him - piano, organ, electric piano, electric harpsichord, two Moog synthesizers and a Mellotron, which can create orchestral sounds of strings, woodwind and brass, in any key, in any combination, from instrumental tapes it contains.

> Signs like 'controllers', 'oscillator bank', 'modifers' litter the electric instruments, which can be combined cunningly by a small digital computer. The music may be fragile and very beautiful; sometimes it suggests several symphony orchestras, an artillery barrage and Dantean screams.

> The creative flair and technical mastery required of him is staggering, enough, perhaps, to make many symphony orchestra section members quail. Yet the level of musical competence is not untypical of the many-stranded music which, for want of a better word (some would say from excess of both prejudice and ignorance), is still called 'popular', with dozens of sub-divisions 'rock' and 'pop'; 'jazz' and 'bubblegum' appended. Such words may, confusingly, hold different meanings for different people. It is easier to call it simply music, the natural music of our century.

For the technical freaks, Rick's instrument collection at this time consisted of: one Custom C_3 Hammond Organ; one Leslie; two Mellotron 400s, one with strings, brass and flutes; and the other custom-made with choir, 'Yes vocals', vibes and other sound effects; two mini Moogs; one RMI electric piano and harpsichord; a grand piano; one digital frequency counter; one custom-built ten-channel stereo mixer and 200-watt monitor system (stereo with amp and cabinets), and Custom pedal board (fuzz, wah, reverb and contour.)

By now touring had got into Rick's blood. And many people think that visiting countries like the States with a super-group must be glamorous, but drummer Bill Bruford put the record straight in a brilliant report from New York during his last tour with *Yes*. He summed up the sub-life of a group on the road to *Melody Maker*.

It was like being in a pod - an insulated capsule containing five musicians, a businessman, a tour manager, three equipment experts, a record producer, a publicist, a man from Atlantic and two tons of electronic wizardry.

And the pod kept leaping from city to city like a jumping bean, stopping just long enough to deliver the goods. Sometimes the pod's walls were hotel walls, sometimes plane walls - or even walls of roadies and managers. The musicians were kept closed off from the world outside.

At each concert, the pod doors opened and the musicians drank thirstily from another culture. Then the capsule was ready to leave again; they were marched back into the pod - and off they leapt.

While they were touring America at this time, Rick had quite a lot on his mind.

Ros was expecting their first child. Rick was in New Jersey when Oliver Wakeman, his 9 lb 11 oz son, was born and was quickly on the phone to the hospital ward where Ros and Oliver were.

Another worry was the constant rumours that had spread like wildfire from New York to Los Angeles that he was leaving *Yes*.

'That hurt a lot at the time,' he recalls. 'When you're on tour, the minute you get into a hotel, everybody phones wives and girlfriends and says "Howya doing?" and all that and when I spoke to Ros she said, "You're leaving." I said "What?" and when I put the phone down and went into the corridor all the group were coming out of their rooms having heard the same thing. It was all over the British music Press.

'What happened, I think, was that at the Academy of Music gig the Mellotron packed up, and the amp as well. Somebody in the audience must have noticed, and the story that "Wakeman refused to play" became "Wakeman's leaving" when it got to California. The band didn't know what was happening and we all freaked out.'

Then something happened that really made Rick think seriously of quitting – his old mate Bill Bruford left to join *King Crimson*. It was a blow because Bill was his type of guy, someone he could loon about with. They had become the Morecambe and Wise of British rock.

'I couldn't believe it,' said Rick. 'I thought the band would crumble. For the first time I had started to feel part of the band, and then it seemed like it was about to end. I admired Bill very much and he didn't go for anything other than musical reasons. He lost the chance of earning a lot of money.'

But Rick admitted that even with Bill in the band he found it difficult to look upon himself as a member of the group. 'I went through a terrible period when I was almost frightened to go on stage, especially in the first half of 1972. I was having a lot of equipment problems and I felt as if people were waiting for me to play a wrong note.'

In an interview with Chris Welch in *Melody Maker* after Alan White joined from Joe Cocker's band as Bruford's replacement, Rick said; 'When Alan came in I was really worried, because it had taken a year for me to settle in. But Alan was great and worked really hard. *Yes* always have to move on for the better.'

Wakeman told Welch how he kept up his own standards. 'I worry about my music. I have to keep on top all the time. I try to be doing something all the time. I'm contented in that I'm doing something I believe in, but I feel I can do better.

'At home I do two hours' practice a day, doing the scales over and over. I'd stopped doing it and it was frightening how hard they were, and how lousy they were - uneven - not good at all. Six or seven years ago I played them spot on. Of all the technical knowledge you get from a classical training, you don't play more than sixty per cent. The other forty per cent gets lost and takes a while to get back. Now I'm thinking of looking up my old piano teacher again.'

Rick had good reason to be a bit paranoid about those early days with *Yes*. The band then apparently showed little sympathy. Jon Anderson said that Rick came into *Yes* as an electronic symphony orchestra. 'We needed some kind of orchestra that we could carry with us, and Rick was the man,' he said. 'All of a sudden he had four keyboards on tour, which kept breaking down. He had to remember all the music.

'We were very unsympathetic in a lot of ways, because that's what he'd taken on. In point of fact, we didn't want him to take on four keyboards, we just wanted him to take on more than one. He took on four, he had a lot of breakdowns, and we weren't that sympathetic. When we came down to playing, we had to carry him a lot of the time.'

Anderson did admit, however; 'But as he developed, he started to carry us at certain points.'

Rick and Jon Anderson during that period were regularly at each other's throats, as were Bruford and Chris Squire. 'I used to row incredibly with Jon in the early days - it was unbelievable, said Rick. 'I could not for the life of me understand where Jon was at and he couldn't for the life of him understand where I was at, but then round about the same time as I began to feel part of the band we all sat down and sorted it all out. I suddenly realized where he was at. At the same time as I realized what I was doing - essentially we were going for the same thing but we just happened to be taking different routes to get there.'

What about the fights? What were they about? 'Silly things really, almost selfishly stupid things when you look back. Like with the equipment I had at the time you couldn't play the Mellotron and the Moog together and hear them both, and Jon'd come off stage and accuse me of not playing something, and I'd say I did. We'd be going hammer and tongs in one room and Chris and Bill would be going hammer and tongs in another . . . but the great thing was that once everyone had got it out of their system it was all forgotten about - till the next night.'

But Jon was the man who finally solved Rick's keyboard problems. 'He suggested that I should get a completely new set of keyboards. I thought that I would just get the same trouble all over again, but I spent £14,000 on a completely new set of instruments, and that made all the difference.' And so Rick became a keyboards' pioneer as the group blazed a show-stopping trail across the States.

It was a hectic schedule, Rick and Brian Lane often took their minds off the worries of touring and turned their attention to their consuming passion - soccer. While Rick is fanatical about Fourth Division Brentford, Lane is just as barmy about First Division Queen's Park Rangers. Lane says he relaxes through football. 'For me, it's pure escapism,' he says. 'Some people take cocaine, I go to football matches.' But there's more to it than that. With his partner Ken Adam, Lane manages some of soccer's top names including George Best, Rodney Marsh, Bobby Moore, Stan Bowles and Gerry Francis.

Rick had been going to Brentford's Griffin Park ground since he was a boy, shouting his idols on from the terraces. But now he decided that he should put his money where his mouth was. So Rick, Brian and Nessui Ertigan, executive of the American club New York Cosmos, and a boss of Atlantic Records, clubbed together to put in a staggering £1 million bid for the West London club, then eighty-fifth of the Football League's ninety-two clubs, planning to make it a soccer Cinderella, by using some of the money they had made from music and their show-business know-how. In return they wanted seats on the board.

'I really desperately wanted to get involved with Brentford and drag them into the 1970s,' said Rick. 'They have been getting tiny crowds for years and all of us who support them have become hungry for success.'

Among the plans the three had was to advertise on the roof of Griffin Park - planes *en route* for Heathrow pass straight overhead - also to advertise so that drivers on the nearby elevated M4 motorway could see, and to buy top-quality players like Bobby Moore, the ex-England captain.

'We had around £500,000 available for players and ground improvements. That would have put the show on the road. The cash ceiling would have been around £1 million,' said Wakeman.

Mr Ertigan, whose father was Turkish Ambassador in Washington, explained at the time he wanted to help Brentford. 'I'd like to take a team from the Fourth Division and bring it up. I know how difficult it is, it's like a dream,' he told the *London Evening Standard*.

'It's really a hobby for us, but it could become important in the future. By persuading good players to come we could build the side. We could use the stadium for many other things. It would be good for the community. Maybe we could have athletic meetings, schools could use it, maybe even rock concerts.'

And those who couldn't believe that Ertigan, an American citizen, was serious soon found out that he is the ultimate in wealthy soccer fans. Besides being a season ticket holder at Queen's Park Rangers, he bought, for 'many thousands of dollars' the franchise to stage soccer in New York City.

Lane said at the time: 'We are prepared to work round the clock to get Brentford off the floor and make them a force at the top.

'This is no pop-world gimmick. We love football and realize we may not have a chance to do something positive.'

But it seems as if Brentford viewed the bid as just that, a pop-world gimmick - and nothing came of it. They are still struggling in the Fourth Division, though Rick is now a Vice-President.

'I was upset the bid didn't work out,' said Rick. 'But despite it, nothing in the world will stop me supporting them. I still go to their games as often as I can. But I guess it may be some time before I can help do for Brentford what they deserve, i.e. 1st division status.'

NINE

Andy Warhol and the 'Six Wives of Henry VIII'

The halting of a controversial television sex film on American pop artist Andy Warhol helped launch Rick Wakeman's first solo album for A&M , 'Six Wives of Henry VIII'.

The album was due to be launched on television on 16th January 1973 - seven days before it went into the shops – with Rick playing excerpts on BBC's *Old Grey Whistle Test*. But because the shock film on Warhol was also scheduled to be shown that night on ITV, it looked as if the audience for the rock show would be tiny.

Then, just hours before the screening of the documentary, journalist and broadcaster Ross McWhirter – later brutally murdered by IRA gunmen - stepped in and gained a temporary injunction banning the screening of the film from three Appeal Court judges.

McWhirter was angry that the Warhol film, made by top fashion photographer David Bailey, included four-letter words and a nude sequence. It also portrayed lesbianism, homosexuality and transvestism. McWhirter said the Independent Broadcasting Authority, watchdog of Britain's Independent television stations, was obliged by Act of Parliament not to offend good taste or decency. Headed by Lord Denning, Master of the Rolls, the high-powered judges agreed the film should not go out and granted the injunction.

Meanwhile, about ten million viewers were preparing to watch the show – many had left the pubs early to see the film that had caused so much controversy – when the late news of the ban came through.

'It seems most of them, rather than watch repeats, switched over to *Whistle Test* and saw my preview of 'Henry', instead,' said Rick. 'And suddenly it seemed as if the whole country had discovered my music. It was a tremendous break.'

The idea for Rick's first solo album for A&M - which can claim to be the world's first instrumental concept album - came about at Richmond Airport, Virginia, when he was on another gruelling *Yes* tour of America.

'I was browsing through the paperbacks on the bookstall when I came across one called *The Private*

Life of Henry VIII. I flicked through it and on the flight to Chicago, I got really interested in the old scoundrel. I quickly finished the book and then got hold of others about him.

'I became quite fascinated with Henry. He seemed to be a very arrogant person who wanted his own way all the time, and I suppose, to an extent, that's how I am. I felt I could identify with him - I don't think I could have lived in those days, but I do like their music. Those were the days when there were a lot of true musicians. There wasn't a place for duff musicians, like today. Actually, I could have only coped with those days if I had been a king or a prince, or someone high up. Because you could only do what you wanted to do if you were rich. And you could only be a good musician if you had the money. Henry was also a man who never forgave anyone for anything. But he was also said to be a competent musician, especially on the lute. Anyway, when I got back from the States I paid a visit to Hampton Court, where Henry used to live, just to get the flavour of the place, the man, and those amazing times. The more I read and researched about old Henry, the more I became interested not only in him, but also his six wives. I was particularly fascinated with their different personalities, and the fate that befell some of them. I couldn't believe that all these women could have been so different - from Anne Boleyn to Catherine Parr, who actually outlived Henry.'

The longer Rick was with *Yes*, the more he struggled to find an outside outlet for his undoubted composing talents. He knew it was fine to be acclaimed as a virtuoso, the world's top keyboard man, but he knew he had more to give. He often scribbled down bits of music as he was travelling, but somehow he could not come up with a theme for a solo album for A&M , who were now anxious to see what he could do.

'I had been searching for a style to write in and suddenly I found it in writing music about these six ladies,' said Rick. 'I couldn't understand why this formula began to work, but it did. I would concentrate on one of the wives and then music just came into my head and I would write it down. Sometimes I was flying, other times I was on stage, or just in front of the piano at home. Quite often I would have a cassette tape recorder handy to tape the results of my composing and listen critically to the playback. The 'Six Wives' theme gave me the thread, the link, I needed to give me a reason for putting these pieces of music together.'

So, with A&M 's approval, Rick began booking studio time and putting tracks about the queens together. Henry VIII was one of history's most colourful characters but he will always be remembered most of all for his six marriages. His first wife was Catherine of Aragon. Because she did not bear him a son, Henry divorced her. After Catherine came Anne Boleyn, Jane Seymour, Anne of Cleves, Catherine Howard and Catherine Parr.

Catherine of Aragon was the youngest child of Ferdinand and Isabella of Spain. She was born in 1485, married to Henry in 1509 and divorced in 1533. Catherine was intelligent, accomplished and spirited although not a ravishing beauty. Henry, anxious for a son to continue the Tudor dynasty, ordered her from court after eighteen years of marriage, having only borne a daughter.

Work began on this track at Trident Studios, London, with engineer Ken Scott, who had worked with many top stars including Bowie. The skeleton music of Catherine of Aragon had originally been called 'Handle with Care', and was written by Rick for the *Yes*, 'Fragile' album. When he began 'Henry', Rick decided to adapt it and use it as the opening track for the record.

'I made a lot of changes from the original 'Handle with Care', and then went into the studio with Ken

OPPOSITE: Rick with his dog Becky

Scott,' recalled Rick.

'Ken is very much what a band needs when it is recording. He is a devil's advocate. If you say, "I'm going to put down this and that", he says, "If you do that, you're going to lose parts on the track." He makes you think about what you're doing and finally you find a way of doing it so that it records properly and comes up with the right sound. Quite often I would play what I considered a perfect piece and he would then say, "I want you to play that again." I would argue and say I didn't see why, but eventually I'd do it again and it would turn out even better.'

Playing with Rick on that track were *Yes* men Chris Squire on bass and Steve Howe on guitar, plus his old pal Bill Bruford on drums, Les Hurdle also on bass, Ray Cooper on percussion, and there were backing vocals from Liza Strike, Judy Powell and Barry St John.

He chose the musicians with great care. For instance, there were four different bass players on the album - because Wakeman thought each was best suited to his particular track. Rick described the Catherine track as 'arranged', because she was a women who had things sorted out.

Next track to be done with Scott, this time at Morgan Studios, was **Anne Boleyn**, based on the tragic life of the French-educated girl who came to the court of King Henry in 1521, where she gained popularity with the younger men. She was of middling stature, with a long neck and beautiful dark eyes. In 1533 she was crowned as Queen. Later she gave birth to a girl - her first and greatest failure. Anne's quick temper and savage tongue broke the spell that had once bound Henry to her and she was executed on 19th May 1536.

A weird dream about her death caused Rick to add a final piece to that beautiful track. 'The night I finished recording 'Anne Boleyn', I went home humming the music, it was really on my mind and I couldn't get it out. That night I dreamed I was at the execution, and, at her funeral service, the hymn, 'The Day Thou Gavest Lord Is Ended' was played. Next morning I went back into the studio and said I wanted to add that hymn to the track. So I did. I found out later that the hymn couldn't have possibly been played at the funeral because it hadn't been written then, but I still think it winds up the track, beautifully.'

Joining Rick on Anne Boleyn was Les Hurdle, bass; Mike Egan, guitar; Bill Bruford, drums; Ray Cooper, percussion; and Liza Strike, Laura Lee, and Sylvia McNeil, on vocals.

By now, Rick was hitting problems as he could only record in between *Yes* tours, which meant there were long time gaps between tracks. He had hoped to complete the album with Ken Scott, but he found Ken was a very busy man.

'He told me one day he was getting heavily involved with lots of other albums and there were problems finding time to continue with 'Henry',' said Rick. 'I got very annoyed because I wanted to get it done and I remember in a fit of rage, I decided to go elsewhere. So I phoned up Morgan Studios and asked if they had any spare time for me. They said they had and so I asked about an engineer. They said they had one called Paul Tregurtha, so I said, "Fine, I'll have him." To be honest I'd never heard of him before and later when I checked with other people, they said I might not like Paul. I asked why, and they said, "Well, he just sits there and does his job. He doesn't talk much."

'How wrong can people be? He turned out to be a great engineer and person, and he's stayed with me for some years. We're as different as chalk and cheese. He describes himself as human, he calls me a yob. But even though we are so different as people we immediately hit it off musically. Paul turned out to be an incredible engineer.'

With Alan Freeman and Brian Lane

So with Tregurtha at the control board, work pushed on. Track three was **Catherine Howard**. Poor Catherine lost her head - literally - in 1542, two years after marrying Henry.

Rick's old friend, Chas Cronk recalls playing bass guitar on the track at Morgan with Wakeman and the rest of the session team - Dave Lambert, guitar; Barry de Souza, drums, Frank Riccotti, percussion, and the one and only Dave Cousins on electric banjo.

'There seemed to be total confusion all around, but Rick knew exactly what he was doing,' said Chas. 'He had Ros scoring out all the parts. She doesn't like music but she was just copying them for everyone. And when we eventually got down to working on the Catherine Howard track I couldn't make head or tail of what we were doing. We were going through it part by part and I couldn't see how all the parts were going to match up.

'Indeed, Catherine switches from the modern to the baroque in an almost moody way, but Rick could perceive everything, right down to the last fader on the mix,' said Chas. 'He knew exactly what he was going to do although he had nothing written down. It was all stored in his head. But he knew what instruments should go on what track. Although it appears confused, everything in his mind was very together.

'And he went ahead and almost mixed that track that night. That was the first time I had seen Rick really working very hard on something like that. He has an incredible ability to store things. Obviously, he knew what he was going to do and had it all thought out, maybe from when he was writing it. He did it right down to the very last over-dub. There are few people who can do that. It's possible to plan the recording of a track up to a point, but I don't think as painstakingly as that.'

Painstaking was right - Rick even went to church to record the organ on the fourth track, **Jane Seymour**. 'I realized I couldn't reproduce the sound I needed on an electronic organ, so we got permission to move the recording equipment into St Giles Church, Cripplegate, London, and I played the massive organ there,' said Rick. 'It was quite an experience playing a lovely instrument like that.'

Queen Jane married Henry in 1536, and died the following year. She was calm, meek and gentle and ready to submit to her sovereign's will. In October 1537, Henry received the son, Prince Edward, he had so ardently desired. Although she never recovered from this birth, Jane was treated more kindly by posterity and was lovingly remembered as the mother of Henry's son. She is the only wife to share the King's grave. Rick played other backing keyboards for the haunting Jane, and the drummer was *Yes* man - Alan White.

The other two tracks were **Anne of Cleves** and **Catherine Parr**. Anne married Henry in 1540. When Catherine Howard appeared it became apparent the King wanted to free himself from Anne and the political and personal obligations therein. It took six months to untie the knot.

Anne graciously accepted the honorary title 'King's sister' and the property that was her compensation, living in comfortable obscurity until 1557. Playing on the funky Anne track were Dave Winter, bass guitar; Mike Egan, guitar; and Frank Riccotti, percussion. Rick thought Anne was a strange lady. 'In fact, she was probably a bit crackers he said. 'And the music is a bit more free.'

Catherine Parr, twice widowed when she married the King, outlived her spouse and later married Thomas Seymour, but she died shortly after giving birth to his child.

Rick brings out her greater maturity and this track is a little more sedate than the others. Playing with Rick on Catherine Parr were Dave Winter, bass guitar; Mike Egan, guitar; and Alan White, drums.

So at last in October 1972, the album was finished. It had not been easy. 'I couldn't get it together,' Rick admits. 'I would record a couple of tracks, go out on tour with *Yes*, and when I came back and listened to the tapes they never sounded right. So I would do it over again and change it. It went on like that.'

Rick went to Madame Tussaud's in London for the album's front-cover picture and was highly amused, when it came out, to see that a wax model of a famous statesman was peeking out from behind Henry and his wives.

'It was none other than Tricky Dicky - President Nixon,' said Rick. 'We decided to leave it in and see if people noticed him. Poor chap, he could do with a few breaks.'

The next big hurdle was to convince A&M that here was a record they could put out. Henry was arguably the first concept album of its kind, being purely instrumental - so it was very much an unknown quantity as far as the record company was concerned. They had to be sure it wouldn't lose a lot of money. So Rick invited Derek Green, British head of the company, to a special playing of the tape at Morgan Studios.

'When I got there the studio was full of empty champagne bottles,' recalled Green. 'I said to Rick, "Do you always work like this?" Anyway Rick played the tape to me and it just knocked me over. It was quite incredible. Shortly afterwards he brought the master tape round to the office for the official play-in and handing over. There were just the two of us in my office and he was really nervous. He was so concerned with my reaction. I listened to it again and again - and it again knocked me out, and for a second I couldn't think how we could exploit it. I just knew it was great. I felt that if there was any justice left in the music business, this just had to get away.

'Rick said to me, "How will you sell it?" I said, "I don't know, but it is really good." We then laid it on for the rest of the staff and they liked it too.' Green added: "My comment now on that superb album was that Rick was really playing from the elbow down, if you know what I mean. I don't know if that will make sense to him. Except that we once spent about three hours arguing that point because he did say that he likes to play from the elbow down. But with that record it was the technique more than anything else that was so apparent. "The virtuosity" is how the music papers might refer to it. I don't really believe that the concept and what it was about was as much a contribution as you might think to its success. I think it was there in the record and it was just down to his ability. And it was right at the time.'

A&M were in for a surprise – a pleasant surprise. They thought the album would sell about 25,000 across the world but they were to be proved wrong. Another testing time was looming. What would the critics say to this departure in the pop world? In fact, the music Press gave it a mixed reception at the time, though now they all agree that the album was a classic and a real trail blazer for today's countless concept albums. Wakeman had started a trend.

Rick was bitter about some of the reviews and once told me: 'Hitler had better reviews after World War II.' He did, however, take note of some of the constructive critics. One reviewer said of the Catherine Howard track: 'This is a good example of an album which is full of good things but is developed no further.'

Wakeman said: 'I thought at the time, "What a cheeky basket," but I really listened to the album again, and that track in particular, and began to realize I could have actually done things to develop the music much further. So since then I have always tried to see what I could do with a piece of music and develop it in every way, even though I may not use a lot of it. I just wanted to see how far I can take each piece.'

Time magazine was quite enthusiastic though. Their reviewer, under the headline of 'Popping the Classics', said:

> Wakeman has conceived, performed and produced what is so far the provocative rock L.P. of the year. The album does not contain literal portraits of Henry's women, rather it is a six-movement instrumental suite conveying Wakeman's musical impressions of the ladies. Devoid of lyrics, it is bursting with diverse sounds; Mellotrons, Moog synthesizers, electric pianos, conventional concert grand, harpsichord, even the 240-year-old pipe organ at St Giles Cripplegate Church. 'Six Wives' is an astonishing classic-rock hybrid that is in the top thirty on U.S. charts, having sold more than 300,000 copies worldwide. Wakeman has liberally drawn on classical style and its techniques in much the same way the Rolling Stones do on blues or The Band on country. For the 'Jane Seymour' movement Wakeman first

recorded an original 4¾-minute toccata on the St Giles Organ, then, back in the studio, he dubbed it over the drums, bass and synthesizer. The result is a bold piece of work - improvisatory, imaginative and thoroughly in keeping with the spirit of the toccatas of Bach that inspired it. In 'Anne Boleyn', Wakeman starts out with the courtly use of an old English hymn, then progresses to a violently free-for-all jazz v, rock v. classics jamboree. In these and the other four movements, Wakeman writes in a manner that has the punch and power of rock combined with the taste and cohesion of traditional symphonic fare.

The writer concluded: 'At the album's present rate of sales, Wakeman should easily gross enough to keep at least his wife from ever having to pull pints again.'

Looking back now on 'Henry' Rick describes it as a 'difficult and cumbersome - yet finally rewarding project'. There was the problem of the stop-start recording between Studio time - it was not inexpensive and before the final mix was completed a large bill had been run up. 'About £25,000 in all,' he said. 'Eventually there was a lot of experimentation done. There were a lot of things we just threw away and money was thrown away. No, that's the wrong word. It wasn't wasted, the money was - invested.

'But because there were no lyrics on the album, I knew that all the attention would be focused on the instrumentation and it had to be good. Otherwise, it'd be detrimental to *Yes*. And there were a lot of *Yes* fans that were going to buy it because they knew we put a lot of work and time and perfection into what we did. If it had been bad, it would have really been detrimental to *Yes*.'

Those fans evidently recognized the skill and effort put into the album, for 'Henry' just sold and sold, reaching number one in the album charts of four different countries. At the last count it had sold more than 1½ million copies.

So a film flop had helped Rick to record success. That Warhol television film was eventually shown. The judges finally decided it could go ahead but the viewers voted it a bore. The country watched it - and yawned, except Rick.

Strangely enough, 'Six Wives', was not Rick's first solo album - he had already 'starred' on a little-known L.P. called 'Piano Vibrations', recorded during his hectic days as a session musician.

It was a middle-of-the-road album with Rick playing Lew Warburton arrangements of hits like Elton John's 'Take Me to the Pilot', Leon Russell's 'Delta Lady', James Taylor's 'Fire and Rain', and the epic 'Cast Your Fate to the Wind', the hit version of which had been made by John Schroeder (opposite) with his own orchestra, *Sounds Orchestral*. The album was released in 1971 and a thank you for his appearance was given to A&M on the Polydor sleeve.

Schroeder, who produced 'Piano Vibrations', was responsible for writing such number-one hits as 'Walkin' Back to Happiness' and 'You Don't Know', and it was he who gave Rick his first solo-album break. The opportunity came when Shroeder conjured up the idea for an Orchestral album series called 'Vibrations'. He takes up the story: 'Polydor were interested and I was launched into producing ten albums on many different themes - Latin Vibrations, TV Vibrations, etc. The idea was partly aimed at tired tycoons. It was meant to be easy listening for the man-about-town, whether married or not, and was ideal for playing on cassettes on the motorways.

'It was 'Piano Vibrations' that enabled me to use Rick as a soloist. 'I knew from previous experience that as a musician he was outstanding; his technique and feeling in his playing was superb. I thought he

was a great talent who ought to be brought to the light in his own right and not lost forever on the session circuit.

'Listening to the disc and the early flying fingers of Wakeman, I could feel his frustration at playing someone else's arrangements, but he still did the job brilliantly. I felt, however, that at any moment his concentration could break and he would then abandon himself to his own interpretation of the music.'

'Piano Vibrations' is still selling around the world - though Rick gets no royalties from the sales. 'I just got a fee of £36 for four sessions it took to make the album,' he said. 'But I am still glad to have been able to make the disc - it gave me invaluable experience.'

TEN

A Bowl of Curry in a Topographic Ocean

No promoter should have the indignity of having a bowl of salad tipped over his head as he walks into a party in Madison Square Garden, New York. Especially after flying 3,000 miles from London to be there. But that's just one of the jolly japes that Rick Wakeman played on hapless Harvey Goldsmith, who has promoted most of his British concerts. The genial Goldsmith had just arrived for a *Yes* party when Wakeman tipped a whole bowl of soggy salad over his head. And as the Thousand Island dressing slowly oozed down his ample body, Goldsmith countered by pouring a bottle of champagne over Wakeman. But Rick had the last laugh. He ordered a commissionaire to escort this 'undesirable character' out of the building. Poor Goldsmith had to return to his five-star New York hotel with the lettuce leaves and dressing still dripping down him.

Rick has established himself as the jester of the pop world with a whole series of hilarious incidents. On another occasion Goldsmith flew into the States to see Rick about business and found him in the bar of a hotel. Wakeman had lined up thirty-six tequilas along the counter and insisted that Harvey start at one end and he the other. They would discuss business when (and if) they met in the middle.

And once Wakeman got the normally teetotal TV presenter Bob Harris so drunk that he eventually finished up unconscious on the floor of the hotel. It was a card game called jacks that caused the problem. A pack is dealt and the first person who gets a jack chooses a drink. The second thinks of an evil combination to put with it, the third pays for it - and the fourth drinks it. It's quite a lethal game, as whispering Bob found to his cost.

But the craziest thing Wakeman ever did while with *Yes* was when he ate a curry on stage in front of a packed house at the Manchester Free Trade Hall.

'I had become so frustrated with playing 'Topographic Oceans', and this night I was really bored on stage,' recalled Rick. 'So I whispered to John Cleary, who looked after my keyboards, "Go and get me a curry, John." He looked rather astonished, but by now had got used to my strange requests.

'Anyway, he returned with the hottest bowl of curry he could get and crawled on stage and slipped it to me from behind the Mellotron. I was playing with one hand and eating the curry with the other. I don't think anyone off stage saw what I was doing because the bowl was covered by my cape, but Jon Anderson smelt it.

'It was hilarious, because part way through the concert, he yelled out, "Eee, I can smell curry." To this day I don't think he knew what I was up to.'

That was the final insult to *Yes*. Rick had become the rebel, the odd man out. If there was ever a king of loners in super-groups, Rick Wakeman would have won the crown. He was a meat-eater in a band of vegetarians. 'I tried health food but it just didn't make me feel full,' he said. He liked propping up bars and chatting to strangers.

Circus, an American magazine, described Wakeman at the time, as 'a worldly soul, a voracious reader, a wanderer in search of new experience in a group that prefers to live entirely within itself'.

Rows about the music and interpretation of 'Topographic Oceans', and how it should be played, came thick and fast. During the first American tour with the band they would furiously discuss new avenues of approach to the piece, and nearly every time there was a four-to-one split - with Wakeman on the short end. Most of the band members preferred Wakeman to enter with an organ instead of a synthesizer at one point in the composition. Once, just as Wakeman was about to go on stage Anderson turned to him and 'laid down the law', about a certain organ passage.

'It would be really helpful,' Anderson said in a stern but reasonable tone, 'if you would swoop right in then and kind of lift us along.'

Wakeman realized he was outnumbered and bowed to the justice of democracy, executing the disputed passage with all the vigorous gusto that's his trademark. Backstage after the show, though, Rick had little to say to the band. Anderson, Chris Squire, Steve Howe and Alan White then retired to a private health food party, while Wakeman chose to remain in the empty hall and talk.

He told a reporter: 'Socially we're not a very tightly knit group but I think it is a good thing that we are that way. When you've got something going for you that works musically it's best that friendship does not get in the way. Sometimes friendships reach a point where they end up being more important than the music. When you're worried about friendships and hurting people's feelings, it's not as likely there will be the free exchange of musical ideas that is necessary for the group to grow.'

Rick's friends began to notice a deep change in him after 'Topographic Oceans' came out. Chas Cronk was one of them. He saw the frustrations that Rick was going through. 'I remember when I met him in New York when they were playing 'Topographic Oceans' at Madison Square Garden,' he said. 'It had gone very well and we were all back stage afterwards because they had a big do with food and drink. And, no offence to anyone in *Yes*, but most of them were posing around looking very swish. And there was Rick with no shirt looking very bedraggled, swigging back the beer. The rest of them were neatly groomed and posing around with all the record company executives while Rick was having a good time. The gap there was obvious really. His first comment to me when I came in was; "Don't eat that rubbish on the table. That's pretend food."'

Derek Green, English boss of A&M recalled another incident: 'I flew to San Francisco to see a *Yes* gig when they were playing "The Winterland" and I went up while they were having dinner. They were all eating at different tables. So I ended up having dinner with Brian Lane and picking up the tab, and they all left for the gig individually. But that doesn't necessarily mean that the band were more untogether than other groups. Obviously groups all have different ways. You are an individual and you have to find individual ways. That's how *Yes* were at that moment in time. While everyone else went off in the limos, Rick had a bottle of beer with the roadies. He always likes to arrive in grand style, does Rick.'

The controversial 'Topographic Oceans' was based on Paramahansa Yogananda's Shastric scriptures, and the esoteric double album made little sense to *Yes* fans weaned on more melodic songs like 'Roundabout' from 'Fragile'. And Rick gave it a rather disparaging nickname. He called it 'Toby's Graphic Go-Kart'.

'To play music you have to understand it. I didn't understand 'Topographic Oceans' at all,' said Rick. 'That's why I hardly played on it. It frustrated me no end - and playing the whole thing on tour, I got further and further away from it. Deep down inside, I don't think I was the only member of the band frustrated on that tour.

'You see, a piece of music, just because it was written several years ago, shouldn't die. Gone are the days when you hear a record for two months and then it just disappears. People are writing pieces of music to last. One of my all-time favourite songs – not just because I played on it – is 'Heart Of the Sunrise' (from 'Fragile'). Incredible tune. 'Long Distance Runaround' - 'I've Seen All Good People' - they're great songs. So why not play them? I felt very sorry for anyone who saw us for the first time on that tour. All they got was 'Topographic Oceans' shovelled down their throats.'

One night, a *Circus* writer wandered into *Yes*'s dressing-room after their set. Eager for feedback, Jon Anderson asked him what he thought of the show. 'I thought it was boring,' the writer replied, matter-of-factly. Howe and Squire quickly joined the confrontation. Howe, who composed some of

'Topographic Oceans', asked, 'What was the problem with it?' 'There weren't enough songs, not enough melodies.' 'Not enough songs?' Anderson was amazed. 'Not enough melodies?' He began singing melodic portions from the piece.

The writer headed for the door. 'Don't ask me how I liked the show,' he said. 'Ask all the kids that walked out half-way through.' When Wakeman heard the story, he chuckled, to hide his true feelings, and wondered why most musicians have no sense of humour. 'The guy had a point anyway,' he said. 'I probably would have walked out half-way through, too.'

Rick added: ''Topographic Oceans' was a guaranteed success even before it was recorded. To go on stage and earn a lot of money from it - well, I felt like we were not only conning people but ripping ourselves off too.

'If you don't enjoy something, and you're getting paid a lot of money for it, then you're cheating not only yourself but the general public as well. I'm more for everything to be worked around melody rather than everything to be worked around clever noises. I really felt bad on the last European tour, and on the American tour. When you are out playing to an audience you have to play what they want, plus a little bit of what you want. You may want to do things they haven't heard before, but you also have to play what they have paid money to come and listen to. For example, we used to play the whole of 'Topographic Oceans', which they all didn't want to listen to. If they wanted to listen to that they could stay at home and play the record. They came to hear all the old favourites, as well as some of the new stuff, of course. And we didn't give it to them. I felt it was a con. Judging by the previous *Yes* tours, I knew how *Yes* could go down, and the rapport we had with the audience. But we didn't have it on the last tour. In Europe, it was an awful feeling for me. 'Yes had always been a band where when we played anything it was almost impossible for anybody else to do it, but on this we were banging things and hitting things that anybody could do and I thought it was degrading for the band. But as was typical of me in those days, whenever I had strong feelings, I'd slip into my little shell, head for the nearest bar, and make matters more unbearable for everybody.'

Despite Rick's feelings about the record, it was a monster success sales-wise. The double album qualified for a gold disc purely on advance orders from record shops. It had an advance of 75,000 - more than their rivals, *Emerson, Lake and Palmer's* 'Brain Salad Surgery', which was a single album - and was the first L.P. to qualify immediately for a British gold disc since regulations were introduced in April 1973 which meant a wholesale order worth £150,000 was necessary for a gold record.

So how did this much maligned album take its shape in the studio? Who did what? Chris Squire told Steve Clarke in the *New Musical Express*: 'Jon had a basic concept. Then, by the time we'd come to rehearse, things that were originally planned got left out, and things that other people thought of - me, Alan, Rick, whatever - got added and the whole thing goes through the *Yes* machine. That's the way we've always seemed to work.'

But despite the problems, *Yes* were still pulling in enormous audiences. For instance they achieved the distinction of being the first rock band to fill London's Rainbow Theatre for five successive nights - the equivalent, numerically, of the London Symphony Orchestra playing the same concert for a week at the Festival Hall to capacity houses.

Tony Palmer wrote in the *Observer*:

> The occasion for this endurance test was the first public performance of the group's epic 'Tales from Topographic Oceans', an eighty-minute, four-movement

work of Wagnerian pretension. Already the piece is being applauded as a masterpiece of contemporary music, classical in structure, mystical in realization. These have not been the only characteristically overblown reactions and, at Tuesday's performance, the players themselves appeared confused as to what was expected of them, the lead singer being unsure whether each section should be described as, for example, the second movement or the second side of the record.

Whatever else 'Tales from Topographic Oceans' may or may not be, it is pop music from first to last, though the music contains much that might be loosely described as jazz, electronic music and Bach-like organ toccatas. Of the four movements, the third, entitled, 'The Ancient - Giants Under the Sun', is of symphonic proportions and structure, and there is a clear attempt at first subject, second subject, development, recapitulation and so forth. The problem seems to be that the thematic material is ordinary and its subsequent elaboration mechanical. No amount of frenzied presentation, spectacular though it was at the Rainbow, could hide the paucity of musical invention.

On their American tour, it was not just Rick's attitude to 'Topographic Oceans' that deflated their spirits, but also the United States Army. The problem arose when *Yes* sought a giant hot-air balloon designed by Donn Miller, a famous balloonist from Atwood, Kansas. The 63-foot-high, coloured orb prominently featured *Yes*'s name, painted on its skin, with graphics by cover artist Roger Dean. The super bubble came complete with radio equipment, two-way telephones, and propane gas burners to heat the air. Hired for roughly £5,000, it was meant to fly all over the country with the group (though in reality the lads travelled by plane), but the gimmick almost tragically backfired.

Besides a pilot to fly the balloon, *Yes* also hired a ground truck to trail around after it and keep everything in order. After the two vehicles left New Mexico all was sailing along smoothly until one afternoon the balloon drifted lazily over a US. Army Base. Though the inoffensive mini-blimp caused only casual interest among the men in olive drab, the truck was halted at the gates of the military reservation and refused admittance. After a few hours, the lone balloonist suddenly realized he'd lost all contact with it and made an emergency landing in the desert in the middle of an Indian reservation. Only after a trek through the sand and sagebush which lasted several hours could he find a telephone booth and call for help.

While Rick's provocative behaviour annoyed his *Yes* colleagues, their health-food fanaticism amazed him even more - like the time they were staying at the Four Seasons Motel in Toronto, Canada. The *Four Seasons* is slightly stuffy, with an emphasis on efficient dining staff and doing everything properly. So the waitresses were a bit taken aback when Jon Anderson pulled out his own loaf of bread, which he gave to one of them to toast. Steve Howe went one better - he'd brought his own jam and cereal. Jon Anderson then ordered poached eggs, 'freshly squeezed' orange juice and milk - plus a bowl of hot water for his cereal and some of Anderson's bread. Squire just ate what the others had ordered.

The waitress was somewhat bemused by all this. 'Are you on a special diet?' she inquired. 'No, it's just better food,' Anderson replied pleasantly.

Jon Anderson once explained: 'We're not really as puritanical as we sound. It's just that when we are on tour we work so hard that we have to be in really good shape to survive. Once we step out on the stage we stay there for two hours twenty minutes, giving all we have got - and that takes an awful lot out of you. When I come off stage my throat is raw and I feel like a crumpled empty cardboard box. If I was knocking back booze and chasing birds I'd never be able to throw all my energy into my music.

We are all so concerned about being on top form that we sleep for an hour before we go on stage. Then I take a dose of honey and lemon just before I go out.' He added: 'Music is our only aim. It isn't compulsory to drink a bottle of brandy a day in order to go on stage and play something that is going to move people.'

But social differences in the group began to underline the other problems. The super success of Rick's solo 'Six Wives' album and later 'Journey' began to bring deep-rooted tensions to the surface.

'At first it didn't matter that we didn't get on socially,' said Rick. 'In fact, when I was in the *Strawbs*, it was our great social life that was the reason for us breaking up. We got on so well that we didn't dare turn to one of the group and say, "You idiot, why didn't you bother to learn your part?" I thought really it was better with *Yes* that we didn't get on socially. And there was another hang-up - at the end of a gig the rest would take their guitars up to their rooms to practise and I was left on my own. I couldn't drag a C_3 Hammond up to the room, though I did have a 'portable' keyboard made. But that turned out to be too cumbersome. At the end of gigs I needed to do something outrageous to alleviate the problems I was experiencing with the band. So I would go to the bar and chat to the journalists and joke with the roadies. In early days as *Yes*, we had a common denominator - our love for the music; but when 'Topographic Oceans' came along, we didn't even have that in common, and we started to drift apart because there was nothing left to grip on to. There was no longer a common goal. My Press friends used to say, "You don't mix with the rest of the band, you're in the bar and they're in their rooms eating vegetarian food."

'But then the Press began to take sides. After 'Journey', several papers said, "Wakeman should get out and do his own thing." Others would say, "Wakeman shouldn't be doing his solo things at all. He's destroying *Yes*." A sort of private war broke out in the Press, and spread to the public and then that interfered with what we were trying to do musically. Admittedly, we had problems, but we were trying to sort them out, and so this kind of publicity didn't help at all.'

Dave Cousins could see the writing on the wall for Rick with *Yes*. 'Rick had got the common touch in that he communicates very easily with the man in the street - which is why he is such a great success in concert. Because he's so ordinary, he's one of the lads. People like that in concert. That was where he stuck out in *Yes*. They were all glamorous superstars. At the end of a concert they walked off with their heads turned aloof from the audience.

'And Rick was down there shaking hands with people in the front row. That was when I saw them in New York. I was totally bored with the music. I had to walk out half-way through and go backstage and get a drink, it was so dull. Rick seemed so out-of-place. He got one solo. And that was a great tragedy because he was brilliant and suddenly the band said: "That is enough of that" - and cut him off.'

Ros remembers a 'terrible night' at London's Inn on the Park, at a reception for the album. 'Rick wasn't at all happy with it and showed it,' she said. 'I was really worried because he looked pale and spent all the time at the bar with rock journalists when he should have been with the rest of us at the sit-down meal. Every time I went over to him, he said; "I won't be a minute." Rick was really unhappy. And he was worried because he agreed with what the Press were saying. He knew what they were saying about the music was true. I remember it had been murder trying to get him along to the studios when they were making 'Topographic Oceans'. I would say: "Rick, aren't you going to the studios today?" And he'd say: "I'll go in a minute." I think he wasn't enthusiastic at all. It was terrible. I think he was worried about it, because he was given no solo parts at all. When you listen to it, you don't hear Rick. He was just blended in. I don't think that pleased him at all. That night, on the way home, he said that he couldn't stay with *Yes* any longer because he wasn't happy with the music they were doing.'

Rick believes a further big problem then was that he had two successful solo albums and 'Journey' had actually hit number one in the charts in Britain. Up until then, *Yes* had not had a number-one album, although they had five top-ten albums in Britain. So Rick took Ros and the family to their Devon farmhouse to try and sort out the problem.

'I knew he was unhappy because Brian Lane kept ringing him and he wouldn't speak to him or ring back,' recalled Ros.

'Every time Brian rang I would have to say, "I'm sorry Brian, but Rick's not here." It got so bad that I told Rick that I wasn't going to answer the phone any more. He could speak to him or do something to sort this situation out. In the end, he sent Brian a telegram. I didn't even know he had sent it. About a day later he said: "I've sent a telegram to say I want to leave the band." It wasn't a surprise, because he was really miserable for those few weeks. After he had done it, I think he felt a lot better.'

Rick told me: 'I could have stayed and earned a lot of money, but I knew then my career had to take another shape. And I knew how much I enjoyed doing my solo projects.'

Yes immediately embarked on the difficult task of finding a replacement for Rick. They finally settled on Swiss musician Patrick Moraz.

Brian Lane, in an interview with the American rock magazine, *Rolling Stone*, shortly afterwards said: 'Patrick Moraz isn't a leader. He's a follower. He'll work out fine. There'll be no problems with him wanting to break out of *Yes*'s confines. Yeah, I think divorce is a good simile to use in describing the break between Rick and *Yes*. When everything dies down and they all run into each other in a restaurant one day, it will be very warm and friendly.'

Rick's comment: 'I seriously doubt if we'll ever meet in a restaurant.'

And Patrick Moraz's comment when he joined *Yes* was a real classic. He was asked, 'Now you've joined *Yes*, will you eat health food?' His reply, says Lane, was, 'If necessary.'

ELEVEN

Journey to the Centre of the Cardiac Arrest Unit

It should have been a happy open-air garden party in South London, but it ended with near tragedy for Rick in a Buckinghamshire hospital. And the 15,000 fans at Rick Wakeman's monster concert at Crystal Palace had no idea how near to death the Caped Crusader was on that summer's day in 1974.

The hospital journey began when Rick decided to try and repeat the success of the Royal Festival Hall concert of 'Journey to the Centre of the Earth'. But this time he was going to make the presentation even more spectacular.

He fixed on the historic Crystal Palace bowl for the performance mainly because of the large crowds it could accommodate. Crystal Palace is a nineteenth-century amusement park, left over from the Great Exhibition of 1851 which was moved from Hyde Park to Penge Park and re-opened on 10th June 1854, by no less a personage than Queen Victoria.

Then completely free of *Yes*, Rick wanted to launch his solo career with a bang, and what better way than with a pop celebration in this famous pleasure spot. He contacted his old pub pals from the *Valiant Trooper* to play again and Ashley Holt, Roger Newell and Barney James were only too pleased to say, 'We're free.' Gary Pickford Hopkins was also available and guitarist Jeffrey Crampton replaced Mick Egan, who was busy at the time - playing for Engelbert Humperdinck. New boy John Hodgson came in on percussion.

'I decided on principle not to hire the London Symphony Orchestra again,' said Rick. 'I felt very bad about the "double pay" incident at the Festival Hall, so I contacted fixer David Katz and asked him to put together a symphony orchestra which I would call the New World Symphony Orchestra. I also hired the English Chamber Choir and we were in business.'

Rick decided he wanted this performance of 'Journey' to be much more visually brilliant than the Festival Hall Concert, and so he presented hapless Harvey Goldsmith with a rather strange demand. 'I want two giant inflatable dinosaurs to go in the lake in front of the stage, and I want them to do battle during the monster sequence,' he said.

Goldsmith, who co-promoted the show with Michael Alfandary, was by now used to bizarre requests from rock stars, and so calmly said: 'O.K. Rick, I'll see what I can do.'

Goldsmith was asked to try and provide a waterfall in the lake. 'I couldn't do that because it would have killed off all the fish,' he explained. 'So instead I put dry ice in the water to create a bubbly effect and then put in some harmless coloured vegetable dyes (blue, green, etc.), to give it colour.'

Preceding Rick at the concert was a formidable line-up, the *Winkies, Wally, Gryphon, Procol Harum* and Leo Sayer, all of whom went down well with the crowd. The stage was set for another landmark in Wakeman's career. But Rick wasn't all set himself. After frenetic rehearsals, he was in desperate physical shape. He hadn't been to bed for five days. Chris Welch recalled: 'The silly lad had fallen over a pile of beer in his local pub just a few days before the show, and had apparently cracked a few bones in his arm. His wrist was bandaged, not a sight to inspire confidence in any sensitive keyboard artist.

He had been warned to lay off for a couple of months, but in the words of the 'Valiant Trooper' – "no way".'

People who saw Rick backstage on the day of the performance, were deeply disturbed at his condition. His mum said: 'We were horrified when we saw him at the Crystal Palace, he arrived late in the afternoon for the concert and he obviously was in pain, and very unwell.' In fact Rick was so ill, that a doctor was summoned to give him morphine to help get him through the gig.

'The trouble started just before the show. I had terrible pains in my chest, and was permanently wringing wet with sweat, and I was losing weight very fast. I told the doctor that I still wanted to go on and he gave me three jabs to kill the pain. It numbed me so completely that when I went on stage I didn't really know what I was doing. I can hardly remember the concert.'

Although Rick finds it hard to recall that day, his fans raved about it for weeks afterwards. He started the show by executing the clashing rhythms of the accident-prone wives of 'Henry VIII' with axe-sharp precision.

The first part featured Rick with his band, sparked by hard-hitting drummer Barney James and wound up to an amusing climax with the 'Big Ben Banjo Band' delivering their 'doo wacka doos' on '12th Street Rag'.

A brief pause followed to enable the New World Symphony Orchestra and the English Chamber Choir to struggle on to the extended, but still diminutive stage, together with narrator David Hemmings and his peacock-throne chair. Rick, clad in white, was looking worried.

Chris Welch wrote in the *Melody Maker*:

> David, in beautifully precise tones, delivered once more the dialogue with faultless diction, and took us in search of Arne Saknussemm's hole, that gaping vent leading from the volcano in Iceland to the Centre of the Earth. It was quite a trip to watch the trees around the lake waving in the evening breeze as the orchestra sent shafts of sound across the silent, attentive mass of huddled jean-clad figures. A vision from the Silurian epoch indeed. Gary Pickford Hopkins, his soft attractive voice blending with the more strident tones of Ashley Holt, took care of the vocal business, while Barney cued in the merging sections of orchestra and group with aplomb. As the extravaganza moved towards the battle of sea monsters on the underground

lake, two floating pieces of plastic began to fill with gas from long tubes, and before our very eyes, took on the shape of prehistoric beasts, several feet high. Cunningly, concealed strings drew them about the surface of the water, and they simulated combat in most effective fashion, while willing hands dumped dry ice into the lake for extra smoke. There wasn't quite the roar of applause one might have expected for this feat of ingenuity, but perhaps the pace of the music precluded interruption. The monsters fixed each other with baleful yellow eyes as 'In the Hall of the Mountain King' signalled the climax.

After such a performance, Rick should have been able to bask in the success at a reception put on in his honour. But by then he was lying semi-conscious in the car as Ros drove him back to their Gerrards Cross home.

Ros recalls the nightmare vividly. 'On the morning of the concert he was bad with diarrhoea. And he was being sick all the time. I thought it was nerves and that he'd be all right in a minute. When he wasn't up by eleven o'clock I got worried and called the doctor. He gave him an injection and some pills to take. Rick was going to wash his hair on the morning of the concert because it was really dirty, but he didn't have any energy. He really felt so lousy. After the injection, he felt a bit better and got out of bed and drove there. We were meant to be going for dinner after the show, but he felt so bad he couldn't. So I drove him home. A few days later his trouble started again. He woke up in bed at about 2am. Adam was in our room at the time; he was waking up for his feed. Then Oliver woke up. So by this time Rick woke me up and I was really annoyed as I was trying to get some sleep. He said, "I can't breathe. I feel as if there's a double-decker bus on my chest." I thought he had probably just had indigestion or something. I said I'd make some tea and give him a Panadol and told him to try and go back to sleep.

'I felt rotten later when I realized what it was. But when he's not well he always puts it on a bit, and I thought he was doing it again. In the end, I realized he wasn't. He finally went back to sleep. Then, that morning he stayed in bed and got up about 11am. and then went back to bed about two o'clock. I thought: "Now, what's wrong?" I went upstairs and he said: "Ros, can you call the doctor?" He couldn't catch his breath at all, and he had a pain in his chest. He looked such a peculiar colour. He looked like cement; really stony and pale. It was horrible. So I telephoned the doctor and told him what was wrong and he came within about five minutes. When he saw him, he called an ambulance, and Rick went to hospital. I went with him. He was really frightened. When the ambulance came, he said: "I don't need a wheelchair - I'll walk." But the ambulancemen said: "No way." So they carried him out and Rick felt really silly because all the band were round here at the time. They were waiting for him to get up. When we were in the ambulance, Rick said: "I don't half feel daft." He was already feeling a bit better.'

But the next part of the trip really freaked Rick out. He takes up the story. 'As I arrived at the hospital I remember all these doctors and nurses around switching devices everywhere. Then they wheeled me down a corridor and pushed me through a door which said, "Cardiac Arrest Unit". And that's what frightened me more than anything else. I turned to the nurse and said: "You've get to be joking." And they started sticking things in me, and they said, "Here you stay."'

Back to Ros: 'They took him into this room for cardiograph readings. Afterwards he said, "I'm O.K. now. Can I go home?" The nurse said they wanted him to stay in for a couple of days, and when she went he felt really fed up. I said: "It's for the best. You're in the right place." He stayed for a couple of weeks. I visited him every day. Apart from his health I had another worry. My sisters and brothers never got on and were always arguing with their husbands or their wives. And I had said to my sister about two months earlier: "Something's got to happen because Rick and I get on too well. Everything's going so smoothly." And when this happened, I thought: "This is it." I felt inside me that everything was going so well. And Rick and I do get on, we rarely have arguments. He's ever so good to me. I just had a premonition that something was going to happen. They told me they thought he'd had a heart attack and this worried me deeply because if it was something to do with the heart I thought he wouldn't be able to work again. And he would be unhappy because he wouldn't be able to do what he had been doing. I know when he goes on tour it's hard work, but I think all musicians who go on tour love going on stage, not only because they're playing the music they want to do, but it's a big ego trip.

'Well, at the time, I thought it could end. And I thought: "What else is there to do? Go into the studio and be a producer?" But he wouldn't be happy doing that all the time. I thought perhaps it was going to finish. What made Rick feel worse was that he was in the heart wing of the hospital. He saw so many people dying as well as those getting better. But other patients said to him: "As long as you do as you are told, and eat when you are meant to eat, and take it easy, and don't overdo it, you'll be O.K."

They told him he was young enough to get over it. I kept thinking to myself how awful it would be if Rick died. I think it's at times like that when you realize how much you love somebody.'

Fortunately Rick started to respond to treatment. 'I was eventually allowed out with the warning to "take it easy", and was given a load of pills, which were to keep me going for the rest of my life,' he said.

'I was really lucky, as I was probably the fittest person in the hospital. While I was there it was not uncommon to see the curtains put round a patient who had just died and then to see him wheeled off. On my first morning home, Ros took me round the shops in the car and when we got back I was so weak that at first I couldn't get out of the car. It was pouring with rain and I stood in the middle of the garden and felt really rotten. I was only allowed to go upstairs once a day. It was all a bit depressing, but I was very grateful to still have my life. Because I like living very much.

'I decided that if I was to survive I would have to look after myself a bit better. But I think human beings are very strange, it works on the same principle as when you wake up in the morning with a giant hangover and you say, "I'm never going to drink again." Two nights later its exactly the same again. When I felt really ill and the doctors said I couldn't do this and that I slowly found myself doing them again, for they were a part of my life.

'For instance, as my strength increased I found myself popping round the pub for a quiet drink and to see my friends. I had given up smoking cigarettes, but then I started smoking cigars instead. My nightmare was beginning to subside.' So did the illness change his philosophy?

'Yes, it's a strange thing, but if you ask any musician: "What would you rather have - your music or your health?" He would say: "I can't live without my music." But if you have come so close to death as I did, you suddenly think about your health, and your family, your friends and everything. Then your music doesn't come first. It does and it doesn't, if you know what I mean. I like living very much indeed.

'There were times when I thought I might never play again. I had silly thoughts. Like when the house was being decorated, and I thought to myself that I wouldn't see its completion. Never go on tour again. It was an awful period.'

Ros recalls how Rick gradually eased himself back into the driving seat. 'He used to sit in the lounge. A couple of days after he came out, he did some arrangements. I suppose really it was good because it gave him something to do. Otherwise he would have been really bored. And then, after a week, he said: "I've got someone to drive me down to the studios. And I'm going to listen to the arrangements I've done." I thought: "Here we go. It's going to start all over again." So I told him to be very careful and to remember what the doctors had said. He said: "I'm only going to sit there." And then, of course, it got a bit more and more.'

For several months the heart attack was a closely guarded secret. *Melody Maker* broke news of Rick's illness like this: 'Rick Wakeman has been in hospital since last week suffering from "nervous and physical exhaustion". But he hopes to be out this week. He was taken into hospital last week after collapsing at his home in Gerrards Cross, Buckinghamshire. The Monday before, said a spokesman, Wakeman had been told to stay indoors.'

The fans did not know that by now Rick Wakeman had made up his mind he could not remain an invalid forever. Heart attack or not, he couldn't bear to be a cabbage. So he decided to make an amazing deal with his doctors. For like the slogan on his favourite tee-shirt said: 'It's too late to stop now.'

TWELVE

'You've All Been Made Part of my Special Loss-sharing Programme'

Rick's deal with a group of top American heart specialists - and a childhood affection for a medieval British king – put him on the road to recovery from his heart attack. According to the textbooks he should have gently eased himself back into active life, but that's not the style of the gentle giant. If he was to go, he would go with a bang, was his philosophy. Otherwise, he would carry on as normal. So he decided to put his band together on a permanent basis, and take 'Journey' and his other music on an exhausting twenty-two-venue month-long tour of the United States.

And he made a deal with his own doctor, who agreed that he could do the tour only if he would work closely with the American heart doctors, who would stand by at each venue. 'I had to get a good heart reading before each show before they'd let me do the concert,' he said. But he added with a smile, 'It's amazing what six free tickets will do.'

Rick made a vital appointment. Funky Fat Fred Randall was engaged as tour manager. Fred, a former merchant seaman, had got to know Rick while chauffeuring Chris Squire around on a *Yes* British tour. Wakeman used to eat with the drivers and they had hit it off together, so Rick decided the well-travelled Randall was just the man to look after the bits and pieces on tour - Wakeman's eleventh of the States, but his first outside *Yes*.

Not content to just take his sextet, he hired musicians from named orchestras in the United States, and called them the National Philharmonic Orchestra, added the Choir of America, David Measham and Royal Shakespeare Company actor Terry Taplin, to do the narration. David Hemmings had to pull out at the last minute due to work commitments. And to carry this vast throng, Rick rented a 105-seater Lockheed Electra aeroplane.

'When I first arrived in New York and began rehearsals with the orchestra, I could see they thought I was joking; just a long-haired nutter. After all, what was a young upstart like me doing hiring them and taking them across the States?' recalled Rick. 'But after a few days we all began to loosen up and they began to enjoy my music. They also began to enjoy themselves - they were drinking as much as us!'

Tour co-ordinator Bob Angles, who was responsible for assembling the orchestra at two weeks' notice, told Cameron Crowe of *Rolling Stone* magazine: 'In most situations where an artist has brought a completely independent orchestra on the road with him, the musicians simply collect their pay and perform with clinical, but detached, perfection. This time the players are so enthused that they're even adding their own embellishments to the music. They think Rick is a genius. They love him.'

The key to the *camaraderie* on that make-or-break tour was that Wakeman was far from the temperamental artiste. He knew the nicknames of the seventy-odd musicians and kept track of romances among members of the orchestra, playfully chiding the blushing participants. The mood was infectious. 'It's like a summer camp and nobody wants to go home,' reported Crowe.

'Rick,' Angles continued, 'is your basic nice guy. He'll never say no. One night he spent a couple of hours in the dressing-room talking with some people like they were old friends. The next morning I asked him who they were. He told me he had no idea.'

A typical venue where the Wakeman circus was a big hit was the UFO-shaped Pittsburgh Arena. There his first set opened with two members from the band - Jeffrey Crampton on guitars, Roger Newell on bass, Barney James on drums, John Hodgson on percussion and Gary Pickford Hopkins and Ashley Holt taking care of the vocals. By the time Rick emerged, only to disappear behind his bank of keyboards, Mellotrons and synthesizers, the Pittsburgh audience went wild. They applauded the various 'Henry VIII' excerpts that made up the first hour's music. A Charleston send-up, complete with four strobe-lit dancing flappers, led into the break.

The second set, reserved entirely for 'Journey to the Centre of the Earth', finally incorporated Measham and company - the choir and orchestra filed on surprisingly smoothly as well as narrator Terry Taplin.

Out of the darkness, in an intentionally melodramatic baritone, Taplin boomed the introduction to Jules Verne's sci-fi classic. Once again the music was well received and the Pittsburgh show, like all the others, got a frenzied, standing ovation. Then came Rick's impish encore, of TV commercials, American style - orchestral embellishments of Chevrolet, Juicy Fruit, Coca-Cola and Bold detergent melodic *spiels*.

But Rick was distressed afterwards. The monitors had exploded halfway into 'Journey', and though the audience did not seem to sense it, the piece became a shambles of blown notes and cues. Measham and Wakeman locked themselves in the dressing-room to debate future policy while changing into street clothes, with Rick, as always, in a tee-shirt and brown leather pants. In character, the exchange was short and simple:

'Next time we'll just stop the show until everything gets fixed,' Rick said, wriggling out of his white cape and pants to reveal blue- and red-spotted briefs. 'The people will understand. They want a decent show too.'

A reviewer from a local paper, sitting silently in the room with his girlfriend, soberly interrupted: 'Why is it that all English rock stars wear print bikini underwear?' 'I don't know,' Rick said to the surprise guest, not missing a chance for a joke. 'Why *IS* it that all English rock stars wear print bikini underwear?' 'No, seriously. Ian Hunter wears the same kind of underwear as you.' 'Don't forget the *Bee Gees*, Pete,' reminded the writer's date. 'Right. The Bee Gees too.' Rick, in a deadpan face, replied: 'I'll tell you something. We all share the same pair. It's worked out great so far, except when the *Bee Gees* stretched them rather badly on their last tour. It's a bit of a tight fit, you know, getting all three Gibb brothers into one pair of print bikini underwear.'

Rick took great pains to make his first solo tour strictly an alcoholic one – no drugs, just booze and more booze. In fact, in the tour programme, he jokingly rated each member of the band by their

drinking abilities.

'I decided early on that I would not allow any member of the band or road crew to take drugs,' he said. 'If I caught them, they would be out immediately. I've seen too much of the results of drug-taking in this business to want to encourage it. Some bands spend all their profits on drugs.' Rick added: 'I admit I do drink a bit, but I believe for all who work for me it must be kept in some moderation, because when we are on tour we are ambassadors not only for the band, but for England.'

And his musical standards were just as high. In the audience at Madison Square Garden was Jerry Moss, joint boss of A&M Records. Derek Green was also there and said: 'I saw Jerry after the show and Jerry, who has seen it all, was really knocked out. He was thrilled by it.' And he added: 'Rick Wakeman's amazing. He's the entertainer of all time.'

'But I'll tell you - one of the things about Rick is that when he got back to London from New York that time I called him up on the day he got back and said: "How was it Rick? I'm so thrilled for you," And he said: "Fine." It was a big tour and he had gone out of his way to do it to promote the record and it had cost him money. Again everybody had said it was impossible but he did it and proved to be right again. And all he said was, "Fine, how is Andy's record?" This was Andy Fairweather Lowe, I couldn't believe it. I said: "It's in the charts." He said: "How's *Hudson-Ford*?" I said: "They're doing great. They're happening with their single." And he went almost down the list with A&M artistes, but with a genuine concern about how they were doing. How were the guys in the office? I was just stunned.'

The tour had been a great success, but like many tours had lost money. The idea is that this will be repaid - with interest - by increased album sales. A compensation for Rick after losing so much cash on the road was the news that he had again been voted by *Melody Maker* readers 'Top International Keyboard Player'.

It's thought Rick lost about £125,000 on the tour. But expenses included the £38,000 to hire the Lockheed Electra, and hotel bills of $3,000 a night for thirty-five nights. Plus wages and the hire of the PA and lights. And, for Rick's prestige it could not have been better. It was a triumph. America had got to know his spectacular music, and he had come through his first big trial without any disastrous health problems.

'There was only one bad cardiograph reading and that was at Houston after a turbulent flight," said Rick. 'After that one I had a rest and we tried again, and this time I was O.K. to go on.'

The more the tour went on the more Rick became a big hit with the orchestra. Flying from Cleveland to New York for the last show, a sell-out of Madison Square Garden, Rick ran up and down the aisles and bellowed, 'I seem to have lost my book on how to shout quietly,' coaxing laughter out of even the more staid orchestra members.

A few minutes later, he decided to say a few words over the PA system. 'First, I want you all to know that I deeply appreciate all your support during the past month. It's been quite an undertaking for all of us. Thank you all, very, very much.' Heartfelt applause. 'Second, I'm sure everybody will be glad to hear that you've all been made part of my special loss-sharing programme.'

For Terry Taplin that last show at the Garden was hot stuff. 'We set fire to his wicker chair right at the end of the performance,' said Rick. 'Poor chap, he must have thought he was on heat .... ' That's the Wakeman way of doing things. Lots of fun for everyone . . . except the recipient of the joke.

As soon as he got back to England, Rick began to joust with his next album - 'The Myths and Legends of King Arthur and the Knights of the Round Table'.

'Strangely, I began putting the music together for 'Arthur' while in the heart ward of the hospital,' said Rick. 'I managed to get a cassette tape recorder sneaked in to me, and when no one was looking, I would hum the music into the mike. You'll never believe the name of the piece I wrote in that hospital - 'The Last Battle'!'

Once again Rick decided to have a large supporting cast and he hired the forty-eight-piece English Chamber Choir, who took part in the live performance of the recording of 'Journey', the eight-piece Nottingham Festival Vocal Group and the forty-five-piece orchestra, again called the New World Symphony Orchestra, and put together by David Katz. Rick's London Symphony Orchestra ban was still in operation, though individual musicians from the famous orchestra did take part.

I went to see Rick during the recording at Morgan Studios and found him in a highly agitated state. We were walking together from the studio to a cafe for something to eat, when he dropped his bottle of heart pills and they spilled out on to the pavement. 'Quickly, find them,' he said, his face twitching nervously. 'I must have my pills.' We found them and he then told me of his life of potential danger. 'I realize how ill I have been and that's why I have to keep taking tablets.' he said. 'But I'm not going to be an invalid.'

Later he spoke about the album's theme. 'There are lots of legends about King Arthur and the Knights of the Round Table,' he said. 'In fact, there must be about 500 books of either fact, fiction or poetry: virtually every famous classical or romantic poet wrote about him at some time. The problem I had was that a lot of the stories and legends differ. Some say Arthur was killed at the battle with Mordred. Some said he wasn`t. Some said he wasn't even there.

'What I did was to choose the stories that I found the most colourful. I read eight books on the subject. A couple of the stories were taken from children's books; writing for children is often far more colourful than in adult books. I picked out four of the most popular stories, and two that aren't so well known. Most of the album is centred around swords, because there were three famous swords which appear throughout the legends. There is Excalibur, which is the sword which came from the Lady of the Lake. There is the sword which was first pulled out of an anvil in the churchyard. The story was that whoever pulled the sword out would become King of England. And Arthur pulled it out. So that is where the whole album starts; how he goes to the churchyard and pulls the sword out to become King of England. Then we do a short track about Excalibur and the Lady of the Lake, which is done with a male-voice choir. And the other sword story is the one with Sir Galahad which is a sword which was floating down the river.

'There is a track about Queen Guinevere, which is old English for "Lady of the moment", which virtually means that every queen he had at the time was called Guinevere. Arthur's body was meant to be found in a tomb at Glastonbury by the monks. And in that tomb were also the bones of the second Queen Guinevere. Guinevere, the one that everyone knows about. has quite a sad story. She had to marry Arthur because he wanted to bring some beauty into the court for the knights. But she loved Sir Lancelot. Every mission or quest Lancelot went on, he dedicated everything to her. There is one story where he goes to what is called the "waste lands", where he has to fight the Black Knight to take over the land. He fights and mortally wounds him. That is actually where my song ends, but the story goes on and he meets a girl there called Elaine, who knows that his love is only for Guinevere.

'But she spikes his drink so that when he recovers consciousness he will fall in love with the first person he sets eyes on. She makes sure she is by his bedside when he wakes up. So Guinevere is very much a love track, because it's sad that she was a woman of great importance, but was very unhappy. Arthur used to think far more about his knights and their quests than about his Queen.'

Rick says he had first become interested in King Arthur as a child. 'There is a little village called Trevalga, which is about six miles from Tintagel, the site which some believe was Arthur's castle. When I was five years old, I stayed down there on a farm for five months and spent a lot of time in Tintagel. It stuck in my mind from then.'

Would he have liked to have lived in those days? 'No, I don't think it was a particularly good era to live in. In fact, I don't think any was particularly good to live in until about the 1960s. Every age up until then suffered from battles and wars. I know there are still wars going on and I'm not altogether a pacifist. In the last war, I would have fought because as often as not, if there is someone or something that is really evil, the only way is to fight. But I wouldn't have liked to live in any age with the threat of war.'

So what sort of man did he imagine Arthur to be? 'Very kindly, but not particularly brave. Merlin used to look after him with all his spells, etc., and Merlin told him he was going to die at the last battle, and never to fight Mordred. He went ahead and fought him, but didn't want to. He knew he was going to lose before he went. I don't think he was particularly brave. I think he lived off the reputation of other knights.'

As in much of Rick's music, there is a fun track, this time Merlin. 'There is a sort of honky-tonk piece which comes twice which is meant to show the light-hearted madness of a magician in a king's court. There's the loony bit with the Moogs which is meant to envisage somebody down in the basement with their big pots stirring away doing all these crazy potions, and there's a little soft melody at the front which is meant to depict one of the legends where he snuffed it at the end. For poor old Merlin, at the advanced age of seventy, fell in love with a mere lass of twenty-five and she returned his love by shutting him up in a cave where he died.'

In the studio many of the musicians gasped when they came to play the last track on side one of the album, Sir Lancelot and the Black Knight. For Rick had written the violin parts so fast that when they came to play them, the usually staid violinists collapsed with laughter. 'Surely, you're joking,' they shouted across to Rick. 'I'm deadly serious,' he replied. They played their parts – after several false starts.

'But twice as fast as I first told them. I thought I'd teach the ones who were cocky sods a lesson,' he said.

As with most recordings, there were times in the studio when nothing seemed to go right, and Rick was getting very frustrated. Then a voice boomed out over the studio intercom: 'Rick, we're having fire practice - you're fired.' And then suddenly came a magical take; everyone beamed. Rick came into the booth to listen to the playback; pronounced himself well pleased; and adjourned to the bar.

Before King Rick and his merry men could go into the studio, they had to wait for the instruments to come back after the tour, and have them repaired. Repaired? 'Yes, the airport freight handlers who shifted our stuff about had an IQ, of about 120 - between them. If you mark something "Fragile", "This Way Up", "Don't Drop", to them that means pick it up upside down, go to the top of the highest building in the area and throw it out of the window,' said Rick. 'Anyway, with the equipment back in working order, we rehearsed the music for about two and half weeks and went into the studios. The preparation was well worth it'.

During the recording, when one of the roadies brought in supplies of fish and chips, Wakeman stopped tinkling the ivories for a moment, grabbed some chips, and said: 'Ere, where's the brown rice?'

Later in an exclusive preview of the new album, Chris Welch under the headline 'Arise Sir Richard!' said:

> Rick Wakeman is rapidly becoming the Cecil B. de Mille of rock. A lover of spectacle and a firm believer in the virtues of simplicity, his new work is bound to receive a roughing up at the hands of cynics. But if one approaches 'Arthur' from the standpoint of entertainment designed to appeal to a wide audience, then one can enjoy this dramatization of the legends in the same way one might appreciate a light-hearted musical or cinema spectacular.
>
> Rick has said he is hoping to create a new kind of light music in which he draws from elements of rock and the classics. His latest project expands on the ideas that made 'Journey to the Centre of the Earth' such a popular success. Bearing in mind this was conceived and executed during a difficult period in Rick's career, when he was beset with ill-health induced by worry and overwork, it is full of surprising energy, and a huge amount of work has gone into the scoring for group, choir and orchestra.

Rick admits he was a bit too ambitious with the album. 'When I first started planning it I told Paul Tregurtha what I wanted to do, and he told me that it was technically impossible. There were just not enough tracks on the recording machine to produce the final required mix.'

But whatever doubts Rick had, the buying public certainly did not - and the music was soon to make Rick into the world's first rock star to present a rock extravaganza on ice.

THIRTEEN

'You Pray — We'll Crap'

The smiling Tokyo promoter bowed politely and smiled at Rick. 'Lick,' he said, 'whatever you do, we will be pleased. You pray, we'll crap.' And 'Lick', who was in Japan for his first tour of the Land of the Rising Sun, had great trouble stifling a laugh at the pronunciation of the oriental gentleman.

Before he went to Japan Rick realized he would need special insurance cover for himself and his equipment. His instruments alone were now worth £85,000 and the gear needed to be transported on tour in two 46-foot articulated lorries, and weighed 17 tons, the total cargo allowed in a Jumbo-jet hold.

So Rick contacted the insurance king of the rock world, Willie Robertson, a music fanatic who always turns up for concerts in a sober pin-striped suit. ('They wouldn't listen to my advice if I wore jeans,' he explained.) Willie who also insures *Yes*, *ELP*, *Pink Floyd*, Elton John and *The Who*, told Rick: 'You'll have to have a medical before I can get you life insurance.' Knowing of Rick's recent medical history he suspected the Harley Street specialist who was to do the examination might be dubious about giving the go-ahead.

'I drove there with Rick and did all I could to calm him down so he would be in the right frame of mind for it,' said ex-public schoolboy Willie. 'I knew how vital it was for him to get the insurance. We chatted in the waiting-room and when he went in he was soon put at ease by the doctor, who turned out to be a Wakeman fan. Rick passed with flying colours and I was able to get him the insurance. By then we were all convinced he had made a rather astonishing recovery.'

Then Willie made Rick into a man with 'million dollar hands'. For each hand is insured for about $500,000. But the insurance policy has meant Rick has had to give up a driving ambition - to go into Formula One motor racing. No insurance company is prepared to take the risk with the cover Rick has on his hands. So he had to be content with sponsorship in the motor-racing field.

'Everyone went potty when I climbed into the seat of a racing car at Brands Hatch,' recalled Rick. 'They were petrified I would damage my hands. So before I could even start to race I had to abandon the idea. No one was willing to the take the risk with a beginner. It was a real drag. I got the bug to drive after seeing the racing greats like Stirling Moss at Brands Hatch years ago. I forgot about it for a

long while until I came to sponsor my own driver. Then the urge came back like a flood. But I daren't go near a racing car in case I gave someone a heart attack.'

Willie Robertson says the insurance policy is especially for pop stars and covers any accident which might stop them performing.

Although he was well on the road to full recovery, Rick kept coming up with plans which caused his advisers palpitations. His first was a mammoth 'King Arthur Day' extravaganza to tie in with the release of the album. Rick thought it would be a great idea to have a medieval pageant, complete with jousting knights, at Tintagel.

'The castle site wasn't really suitable so I suggested a giant-sized blow-up castle in a nearby field, to take its place,' said Rick. So Harvey Goldsmith was dispatched to Cornwall to try and organize the 'do'. He found the land was Crown Property and after a series of letters to the Duchy of Cornwall, which brought little response, it was decided to leave old Arthur alone in that lonely county.

The record itself got tremendous reviews and Rick was certainly not discouraged by the problems at Tintagel. He suggested they use Wembley Stadium, England's largest soccer arena, for a special presentation of 'Arthur'. 'He wanted so many people to take part that we thought we could fit them all in on the terraces and have the audience on stage,' said Goldsmith, tongue in cheek.

So the famed stadium was also out. But the Caped Crusader does not give up that easily, and finally he had his way on ice. He plumped for the place next door, The Empire Pool, Wembley, for an ice spectacular of 'Arthur'. This time he hired the fifty-eight-piece New World Symphony Orchestra, the forty-eight members of the English Chamber Choir, the Nottingham Festival Singers, the *English Rock Ensemble* and nineteen ice skaters.

'We're building a castle in the middle of the stadium with a drawbridge at either end, and the skaters - they've all been choreographed - will act out the parts. The sound at Wembley is notoriously bad so I've imported a very intricate American PA system which means that every instrument on stage has its own method of amplification. The audience won't miss a note,' he told the *Sunday Times*.

The reporter commented: 'It sounds like the grandiose kind of folly which only a millionaire pop star could or would perpetrate. But twenty-five-year-old Wakeman - a superb rock organist – has a habit of attempting what seems impossible and turning it to profit.'

Rick said: 'I'm not daunted by big shows. You have to push past the scepticism and persuade people it can be done. If you do it once then forever after you'll get all the support you need. On the other hand if you try to hype your way through a situation you always lose. When we did 'Journey' we lost a bit on the concerts, but we made it up in record sales. It was in the top ten for twenty-three weeks.'

As the band rehearsed, Harvey Goldsmith worked feverishly to put the project together. 'One of the troubles with being an ideas man is that you then have to work them out,' he said a couple of days before the first night of the three-night run. 'We have a round stage like a castle in the middle, with a drawbridge to get the musicians over the ice. But then there was the problem of having a round stage in a rectangular area. It would mean that people couldn't see what was going on at the opposite side. So we're duplicating the action, and it [skating] will be done simultaneously at both ends.'

The three shows were seen by 27,000 people and many millions of others on television, because one show was recorded for later screening. Despite first-night teething problems with the sound equipment, Rick received warm reviews.

Since then the 'King Arthur' album has been put to more good use with Rick's racehorse - Tropical Saint. For the horse was exercised in Oxfordshire by TV personality Michael Wale - to a tape recording of the music. 'It helps the horses get used to different sounds at race meetings,' explained Mike.

Rick decided to buy his first horse - Tropical Saint - when he realized he was getting too intense in his music. 'I was getting no relaxation at all and this wasn't good for me,' he said.

So he got together with racing fanatic Wale and they went to see Captain Charles Radclyffe, who buys and sells yearlings from Ireland.

'We didn't exactly call at the most as opportune moment,' remembers Michael Wale. 'For when we arrived we found there had been a fire at the Captain's house in the morning and there were police and firemen everywhere. Anyway, he and Rick got on very well and Rick bought a three-year-old horse. The next problem was thinking of a name and colours for it. Rick finally came up with the colours of Tropical and the name of Saint. It ran for the first time at a steeplechase at Newbury in 1975 and came seventh out of twenty-three. Not a bad start.'

The horse was trained by John Webber in Oxfordshire, and ridden by his son Anthony. His colours are: purple, black cross of Lorraine, brown and purple hooped sleeves, brown cap with purple diamond. It never won a race and died in June, 1977, but was placed third out of nineteen runners at Worcester in November 1976 at 20-1. Rick did not arrive in time for that race, but he placed his bet *en route*, at a bookies in Cheltenham - and was overjoyed to find the Saint figuring in the frame when he finally reached the track.

As he continued to build up his amazing collection of musical equipment, Rick found it more and more difficult to store it in a double garage of his home. So he looked around for a nearby warehouse where he could put it all. 'I eventually found a recently built factory on the Abercromby Industrial Estate in High Wycombe. It came on the market at the right price but was really too big for my needs,' said Rick. 'So I thought about making use of the surplus space. I thought of all the money I had been forking out for rehearsal rooms, so I decided to build a couple at the factory. When I was not using them, I let them out to other groups. I was also paying out a small fortune for flight cases to pack my equipment in, so I thought, 'Why not start a flight-case business as well? I can make my own, and then sell to other groups.' So I did. It has now snow-balled and I had seven companies there. I called the place Complex Seven. I've now moved to other premises nearby.'

Rick's firms are:

- C.7 Leasing Ltd: for the hire of musical instruments, etc. including a full lighting rig with operators.

- C.7 Studios Ltd: two well-equipped rehearsal studios.

- Voustar Ltd: the marketing and sales of various developments by Shandbest and Helpinstill piano pick-ups.

- Packhorse Case Co. Ltd: manufacture of flight and protective cases.

- Birontronics Ltd: production of a new and versatile form of keyboard instrument.

- Shandbest Ltd: research and development company to produce prototype musical instruments for professional musicians.

- Rick Wakeman Ltd: this company looks after Rick in his touring, Press and publicity outlets.

In the early days of the company there was an amusing incident when Rick turned up at Complex Seven. 'One of the women there didn't recognize me and said, "Can I help you, sir?" I said, "No it's all right, I'm just looking round." She persisted, "I'm sure I can help you sir." "No, it's O.K." By this time she was getting worried with this long-haired monster roaming around the place without explanation. "Who are you, sir?" she finally asked. "I'm the chairman," I said.'

Fred Randall describes Rick as a 'clever but headstrong businessman'. Fred added: 'He frightens me sometimes. He has an exceptional mind for figures. He can add them up quicker in his mind than I can using a calculator. Rick knows everything that's going on, but won't interfere with the people running things. He has a way of dealing with employees by suggesting they do things, rather than telling them directly. He looks upon the companies as a safeguard for the future and a way of keeping some of his mates in work. The business will be for Oliver and Adam, his two sons, one day.'

With 'Arthur' selling well, and his venture into the commercial world coming along nicely, Rick had time for a new move - into the film business. And for this he teamed up with another larger-than-life character. Ken Russell has always been a bit of a shocker. He shocked some film fans with *Women in Love* and *The Devils* and others were taken aback by *The Music Lovers* and *Tommy*. But with *Lisztomania* he took the ultimate step, proving that it is possible to shock all the people all at one time.

And because of the film - and the soundtrack – 'produced and arranged' by Rick, which accompanies scenes of rape, exorcism and blood-sucking, the pair were 'black-Liszted' by the Liszt Society. The trouble began when Mrs Eunace Mistarz, the Society's Secretary, sneaked into a theatre to watch the filming of the life story of her hero, the nineteenth-century Hungarian classical composer Franz Liszt. Then came the surprises: there was Liszt, played by Roger Daltrey, sitting at the piano - with girls in Victorian bonnets screaming 'Chopsticks'.

'I was amazed,' said Mrs Mistarz. 'Daltrey was pretending to play the piano while one of Liszt's compositions, a variation of the tune 'Chopsticks' was being dubbed over. They were making a mockery of the composer.'

Mrs Mistarz was said by the *Sunday People* to be so angry that she had called a meeting of the Liszt

Society, among whose members were renowned intellectuals including Sacheverel Sitwell and famous musicians such as Yehudi Menuhin.

But that scene was mild compared with others in the film in which Franz Liszt emerges as a sort of sex-mad nineteenth-century *Bay City Roller*. Wagner, who was played by Paul Nicholas, was portrayed as a vampire and as Hitler. Then there was Ringo Starr who played the Pope, wearing spurs and speaking with a Liverpudlian accent, plus sex - and organs (of the human type and of every size).

But what surprised Wakeman fans even more was the acting part he was given by the bizarre Mr Russell. Rick explained to Chris Welch, 'Ken called me into his room one day at Shepperton Studios, and said, "Wagner creates a god in this, which he wants to go out and conquer the world. It's got to be the god Thor, a guy with incredibly long, blond hair. 'He said, "Go down and see make-up. You're on, on Monday." So seven o'clock Monday morning, seven every day for several days, I'm there, and somebody says: "Here you've got to be sprayed silver."

'And this guy says: "Right, take off all your clothes," and he sprays me all over and I am then given a big winged helmet and a mauve leotard. Ken then tells me: "It's very easy. All you've got to do is lie still. Wagner comes in with Liszt and says he's got a monster to go out and conquer the world, and he pulls back a sheet and you're lying on the operating table. Just lie there." 'So for two days I just lay there. Then he thought I ought to come to life. "You're a drinking man, aren't you? Give him a pint of Heineken to bring him to life." So Wagner gives me a pint of lager and says: "What charm, what grace - masterful man." I give a huge belch. We used proper lager. And we did twenty-seven takes.

"I was out of my box. I was not a well man. Then Ken said: "You can't just sit there. Get up, walk through the French windows and conquer the world. No, wait a minute! That would be boring, really boring. As you walk towards the French windows, stop by the fire and pee in it. And put the fire out."

'I said, "Listen Ken, I can't guarantee that. I'll do the belches all right, and drink as many pints as you want. But I can't guarantee on managing to pee on the fire every time." So Ken said, "That's all right, I've got something made for you - a huge silver whatsit." And they stuffed it down my trousers and I'm peeing on this fire amidst the flames. Wagner then knees me in the nuts and that was the end of my screen debut. It was ludicrous but marvellous.' Rick added: 'It was not quite the screen debut my mother had in mind for me. And I guess it nearly sent Mary Whitehouse to her grave.'

So how did Rick get involved in such a strange way-out film? 'Basically the person I have to thank for that is a guy called Bill Curbishley, who manages Roger Daltrey. There was one song that had to be done and Ken, who normally used to use pre-recorded tapes for his soundtracks, decided that this song he wanted done differently and Bill suggested then that I did the song. I did and he liked it, so he gave me another bit to do and finally I ended up doing the lot. Ken Russell is an amazing person - a genius. He's as sane as I am, and you can take that as you wish. No, I like the man very much. He's a doer not a thinker. I like doers. Anybody can think. Some people say he's absolutely mad. I think he's most probably incredibly sane, in a strange way.'

Rick's view of the film: 'I enjoyed doing it and I loved each section as it was being done, but I wasn't sure what I thought when they were all stuck together.' So what was the Russell-Wakeman vision of Franz Liszt? 'Well, the way I look at it is that if you could take a circle and on the outside of the circle, you started Liszt and you looked at him deadly serious, then you exaggerate it a little bit to make it almost corny, then you exaggerate it a bit further so that all the different elements of say the horror that came into his life were exaggerated going on until in the end you almost do a full circle which is going to the absolute sublime, almost to the ridiculous, but it still bears that resemblance, it is really an outrageous version of the true story and I tried to do the same with the music,' said Rick.

'Liszt and Wagner are the two main composers in the film and I tried to put myself in their place in the twentieth century and tried to imagine if I had just written the music that they had written how I would orchestrate it, knowing that I had now got the electrical and technological advances of today. Some worked, and some didn't, but overall, considering all the circumstances, I feel I gave all I had.'

Chris Welch writing in *Melody Maker*, assessed the album, like this:

> It's an odd album, with that two-dimensional feeling of a soundtrack sans vision, in other words, it would help to see the movie. Wakeman has produced all the tracks, some of which feature the powerful tearing vocals of Roger Daltrey, the high-note whoops of that unlikely Rhine maiden, Linda Lewis, and the narrative of Paul Nicholas, as the evil Wagner who plays on Roger Daltrey in his new role Franz Liszt. Nicholas, you will remember, was the evil Cousin Kevin who preyed on Roger Daltrey in *Tommy*.
>
> The music, freely adapted from Liszt, Wagner and Teresa Brewer, is a bizarre (how else) mixture of the grandiose, banal and episodic. Moments of Wagnerian drama cannot be disguised, although Liszt's themes seem to suffer most in the interest of pop art.
>
> Liebstraum becomes 'Love's Dream' set to a twist beat, trombones evoking intoxication; while a comic music for all melody tantalizingly recalls such past hits as 'Music, Music, Music'.
>
> But there are moments of real power, and Rick is given free reign for keyboard expression in a way he has not enjoyed since his first solo album, 'The Six Wives of Henry VIII'. The banality of some of the performances is intentional, since the movie is a parody but I preferred the blitzing power of pieces like 'Master Race' and 'Wagner's Dream', the surrealistic invention of 'Hell', and the thundering imagery of 'Rape, Pillage and Clap'. Russell and Wakeman seem an odd creative partnership, and one that will be exposed to heavy abuse, but amidst all the bad taste and sensationalism, they produce something brutal and honest.

But Rick, in a moment of despair, later told me he hated the soundtrack album. 'I thought it was dreadful, truly awful,' he confessed. 'It was nothing to do with me. There was hardly anything of mine on it in the end. I only played on a few minutes of it. I thought it was appallingly mixed and dreadfully produced. They stuck my name on it as producer but I never produced it. I wasn't even in the studio when they did it. One day I'll release some of the stuff which I wrote and played which I thought was good and should have come out. It was not used on the album for certain reasons. And the rows had gone on so long, I just said, "Here are all the tapes, do it yourself. Take my name off it, and do what you like." And I added: "I warn you now, you will balls it up." And they did. But that's water under the bridge.'

He was so angry about this incident and determined it would not happen again, that he made a special trip across the Atlantic. 'I made my words felt with A&M ' he said. 'I flew over to L.A. via New York and had a long meeting with my New York lawyer, and told him exactly what I thought. And he passed on the message and it was sorted out from there.'

A new feeling had joined the Wakeman senses - bitterness.

FOURTEEN

'My Name's Ronnie Biggs — Can I Have a Couple of Tickets?'

Ronald Biggs is no ordinary rock fan. He was a key member of that elusive band of villains who brought off the £2,631,000 Great Train Robbery in 1963. Ronnie got thirty years for his part in the raid, but two years after being sentenced he was 'sprung' from London's Wandsworth jail. That was the start of an astonishing escape route which took him to the Continent, Australia and finally Brazil.

Biggs now lives in the South American sunshine of the fishing village of Sepetiba, forty miles from downtown Rio de Janeiro, and is the father of Michael Fernand de Castro, born in 1974 to Raimunda Nascimento de Castro, a Portuguese Indian. The birth of his son meant that the Brazilian Government would not allow him to be deported to Britain.

Life for Biggs, however, does not seem to have the same sparkle of the waves off Copacabana beach. His wife Charmain - mother of their two sons - has divorced him. 'I am stateless, I'm broke and I've lost the wife and family I loved,' he says.

And the world's most wanted man cannot work or drink alcohol and usually has to be indoors by 10pm. So his social life at most times, is completely non-existent.

But it changed for a few hours when Rick Wakeman went to Brazil with the English Rock Ensemble to perform excerpts from his albums with the Brazilian Symphony Orchestra laid on especially for him by the country's government. For in Brazil, Rick is hailed as one of the world's top composers. He is feted everywhere he goes.

While in the coffee country, where Wakeman and the boys played to about 500,000 people, Rick took a phone call at his Rio hotel suite.

'Hello, is that Rick Wakeman?' said the Cockney voice. 'Well, I thought you'd be glad to hear an English accent. This is - Ronnie Biggs, do you think you could fix me up with a couple of tickets?'

Rick was a bit taken aback by the directness of Biggs's request but took a deep breath, and said: 'Certainly Ronnie, I'll fix it.'

Fascinated to hear from such an infamous crook, Rick arranged to meet him for a meal, and later they went to the races. 'We got on very well and Biggs boasted about his part in the "crime of the century",' said Rick. 'He hinted to me that the real truth about the hold-up has never been told and said he wanted to make a film about the robbery. He asked me to do the soundtrack.

'Biggs then gave me a present – the shirt he said he wore for the robbery. I gave him the shirt I said I wore for my wedding.'

Did Biggs enjoy the concert? 'He was really knocked out with it,' said Rick. 'He told me it was the most enjoyable thing that had happened to him since Detective Inspector Jack Slipper, who had flown from London to Brazil to arrest him, admitted defeat and went back home!' That hit Brazilian tour got off to a bizarre start with a phone call from the promoter to Rick at his Buckinghamshire home.

'He phoned from Brazil and asked if there was anything he could do to make my visit more pleasant,' said Rick. 'For a laugh, I told him I wanted fifteen virgins who had all won beauty contests to be brought to my hotel room when I arrived. I thought nothing more of it - but when I arrived at the hotel I found a queue of nubile young ladies outside my bedroom. And the Press heard about it, and splashed the "strange sex habits of Europe's rock play-boy".'

Still, it kept the roadies happy.

While Rick believes in taking touring seriously, he also understands that if the strains and stresses are not relieved from time to time, there will be problems. So he makes sure there is lots of fun along the way for his travelling companions – and the audiences. While touring Australia, he came up with an idea for an encore that was to gently send-up the Aussies. He sent out Fred to get eight grass skirts, eight wobble boards and eight Rolf Harris masks. Funky Fred got the skirts and boards but he found no one made Rolf Harris masks. 'I'm not really surprised,' said Rick. And at the end of the show, the road crew brought the house down as they wobbled their way through 'Tie Me Kangaroo Down Sport'.

When the band flew on to New Zealand they had to leave the skirts behind because of the health laws banning the import of plants. But that did not beat Fred. He ripped down some of the plastic sheeting over the open-air stage in Auckland, cut it into strips, and the roadies wore plastic 'grass' skirts.

Orchestral manager Bob Angles was the target for lots of the jokes. Especially when they were staying in Sydney's poshest hotel, when Rick decided Bob was not eating enough. 'As I went to bed one night I saw Bob had ticked off one or two items on the breakfast list outside his room, so I decided he might like a couple more boiled eggs and two or three rounds of toast,' said Rick.

'Then when Ashley came up he ticked off a few more, and Budgie and the others did the same. When I got up next morning eight waiters were heading for Bob's door, heavily laden with plates. Next minute I heard Bob desperately saying, "I never ordered all this." And the head waiter was saying, "It's all ticked off here, sir - and that'll be $194."

'One day we roped Bob in for the grass-skirt encore. He took a lot of bribing, but eventually he stripped off. When we got back later he couldn't find his clothes anywhere. He came into my dressing-room and said, "Someone's hidden my clothes. I don't suppose you know who it is? I'm going to see he pays for this." I told him, "Yes, I do know, it was me, and at the moment they are on their way back to the hotel." He had to go back in a taxi and walk through the foyer clad only in a grass skirt.'

Narrator Terry Taplin, too, had more than the audience to contend with. 'Terry told us that in the Royal

Rick's Brazilian tour. Above: receiving a golden disc for 'King Arthur'
Below: a knees-up with Brazilian 'record people'

Above: Rick (and two discreet bodyguards) watch the semi-final of the Brazilian Cup
Below: The road crew and band with Rick's Brazil team before their charity match

Shakespeare Company there is a tradition that if someone is on stage and hears "Phht" he has to act as if he has just been shot in the back with an arrow without the audience knowing. So we used to try it out on him when he was narrating "Journey". Some nights it would put Terry off his words and mistakes like "Mount Etna" being pronounced as "Aunt Edna" would occur.

'Every night Terry would take a cup of water on stage for his throat. One day we filled it with Thousand Island dressing and of course he drank the lot without looking. It completely clammed his mouth up. Another night, just as he was coming to the part about the "frightening Mount Etna", we set fire to his chair which was meanwhile lifted up in a fork-lift truck."

Singer Ashley Holt says some of Rick's tricks could be extremely painful. 'Quite often the band would come off stage dying to go to the loo, and just as we were about to relieve ourselves, he would yell, "Come on lads, we're doing an encore." We'd have to rush back on stage. You imagine trying to smile at 20,000 people and sing when you're in agony. I used to cross my legs, grimace, and somehow carry on. Oh, well, that's showbiz.'

Drinking as usual played a large part in this mad tour of Australia, and an excess of it later sent percussion man John Hodgson on a journey he will never forget. 'John had been out drinking in Sydney and had had a little too much,' recalled Rick. 'Two of the road crew took him back to the hotel, put him in the lift, told him his room was on the eleventh floor, and he must get out when the doors opened. They pressed the button and went back to the club.

'When the rest of us got back to the hotel at four o'clock in the morning, we found Hodgie still propped up against the wall of the lift. He'd been going up and down all night. He tried to explain that every time the doors opened he hadn't been quick enough to get out!'

Rick is a person who hates to be beaten on anything. So when a group of hard-drinking New Zealanders challenged him and the band to an on stage 'World Championship' drinking contest, he told Fred: 'Fix it that we win, or else.'

So Fred doctored the opposition's share of the local brew, supplementing it with shaving cream. 'Of course we won hands down,' said a triumphant Rick. 'Fred had done it again.'

But it was during a late-night radio chat-show in Australia when Funky Fred finally achieved nationwide fame. Up until then he had just been Rick's backroom boy, the original Mr Fix-it.

'When we flew into Australia for the first time Fred peered out of the window of the jet, and said: "Washy will be down there waiting to greet us with a barrel of beer." Apparently, Washy was an old mate from Fred's merchant navy days, who had emigrated to Australia,' said Rick. 'Everywhere we went Fred expected this bloke Washy to be on the tarmac, but he never was. So every night in every hotel Fred would go through the phone book ringing up everyone called Washington he could find. It got absolutely ridiculous.

'Anyway, it got to our last date, in Sydney, and there was still no sign of him. I had to do this chat-show and Fred was still muttering about the mysterious "Washy" when suddenly he dived into the studio, grabbed the microphone and said: "Washy, wherever you are, this is Fred Randall. I've been looking everywhere for you. I'm at the studio. Bring the beer." Then, with a smile, he sat down. End of interview - Fred had stolen the show.' Wherever Washy was he obviously didn't listen to that station – for Fred didn't hear from him!

Conductor David Measham was another unfortunate victim on tour. 'One night we taped up the rostrum so David had trouble getting on it,' recalled Rick. 'We started playing just as he was half-way there and he ended up conducting with one leg on the rostrum and one leg off. And we stuck the pages of his music together, as well, and swopped his baton for the biggest drumstick we could find.

'We also tied a handkerchief on to the first violinist's bow so that it tickled his nose.

'The audience usually didn't know what was going on - it was a private joke. But one night they had a laugh when we stuck a notice on David's back which read, "I am the conductor", which I thought was very funny until I came off, took off my cape and found the band had stuck one on my back which said, "This is the star".'

Before Rick arrives at each new venue, a lot of work has been done. And that is where the serious side comes in. For Wakeman is very thorough in his research.

'Before I go, I get copies of local papers sent to me and read them from cover to cover. I try and find out local happenings and anything that we can make fun of. I feel that if people 12,000 miles away have bothered to find out a bit about me, the least I can do is to find out a little about them. It helps me get into their environment and try and understand it, and for a day I virtually become a citizen of their town. I know all about them when I arrive.'

Rick has two golden rules when he goes on stage - the first is if he does not like the place he doesn't slag it off. 'After all,' he says, 'it's not the people's fault.' The other is that he doesn't always say, 'This is my favourite town in America,' or wherever he is at the time, just changing the name each night.

'For the non-English-speaking countries, Rick learns a bit of the language. He knows sixty sentences in Portuguese and forty in Japanese. Audiences in Japan loved Rick and his merry men and on his first tour there he decided to introduce some of the numbers in their own tongue. So he got someone to translate sentences like: 'I'm really pleased to be here. I'm sorry my Japanese is so bad.' And then, he tried them out on one of the organizers. The inscrutable expression disappeared from the man's face.

'Was that all right?' said Rick anxiously. 'The Japanese was great, Lick,' he replied, 'but I don't think audience will understand why you say, "Girl in front row has big tits." So Rick hurriedly found a different translator.

In the Land of the Rising Sun, there is no slapstick during Rick's performances. 'There I'm treated very much as a classical composer. The audience turns up in tuxedos and bow ties, and the youngsters dress up too, which they don't normally do for rock concerts,' said Rick. 'So we play the whole thing straight.'

Off stage, however, there is still lots of fun. Like the night King Records bosses - that is Rick's record company in Japan - took Rick and Alex Scott, Brian Lane's right-hand man, out to dinner.

The evening got off to a bad start because Rick forgot that you had to take your shoes off in the restaurant - and he was not wearing any socks. 'My feet smelt like a Turkish taxi driver's armpits,' he said. 'Our translator that night was a young Japanese girl who spent the whole evening with a red face. It all began when I remarked to Alex, "Isn't it funny how Japanese girls all have little tits." One of the record bosses wanted a translation of what I had just said. The poor girl spent the next hour and a half translating rude words from Japanese to English and back again. It was hysterical - but successful, because I immediately re-signed with them for a new five-year contract!'

But it was Rick who had a red face one night in America when he ripped his trousers badly and signalled Fred to bring him on a new pair. The concert was stopped for a few minutes while he changed them behind his cape. Fred then left the old ones in the wings and Rick was very angry later to find that a fan had vaulted the barrier and stolen them. Brian Lane put out a £50 reward for their return and finally got them back. 'But they were in such a bad state I couldn't wear them again,' said Rick.

In fact, some nights the audience want to take over the comedy and it could turn nasty, but Rick always gets the last word. He deals with hecklers in his own inimitable way. 'Some clown might shout out: "Give us some rock 'n' roll." And I'll say something like, "Could you keep your mouth open please, there's a Greyhound bus that's looking for somewhere to park." Then I launch straight into the next number and he's finished for the night.'

Joking is a way of life off stage, but the minute Rick sets foot on the boards, his mood is deadly serious. 'My mind goes blank. I'm completely obsessed with playing,' he said. 'If I wasn't, I'd do something wrong. If you forget one knob on the keyboards, you panic. It's a funny feeling being on stage. I really can't describe it. If it's right, it's the closest thing to heaven, a kind of factual dream, the ultimate in happiness. When it goes wrong it's a natural low.'

Observed Fred: 'Rick comes alive on stage. It's as if someone throws a switch. He gets so involved with what he is doing, it is obvious to everyone around him.' For once the clown is playing Hamlet.

FIFTEEN

On the Trail of a Spaceman

While Rick was writing his mysterious album 'No Earthly Connection', he may have had a UFO watching over him. For what he says looked like a spaceship swerved across the sky in Miami in the area of the infamous Bermuda Triangle, and hovered long enough for him to summon Roger Newell, his bass player and a confirmed star watcher, as a witness. For a moment the UFO hovered, then shot away into the distant sky as the two men watched dumbfounded.

'It did a zigzag across the sky, shot up and vanished,' said Rick. 'Even now I hesitate to mention the incident because I don't know if anyone will believe me. But a local Miami paper next day confirmed what we saw. They carried news of the UFO sighting by other people.

'I knew at the time everyone would explain it away by saying that the pressure of writing the album was getting me down; making me imagine things. When I first noticed it, I thought it was a shooting star. But no shooting star falls across the sky, stays still for an hour and then shoots off in the other direction.'

The incident took place at 3am. while Rick was writing on the veranda of a beach house in Florida, overlooking the triangle of water which has apparently been gulping up planes for years. His fascination for the unknown had gripped him so strongly during that tour of America, that he carried notebooks and pens wherever he went, scribbling down the themes and melodies as they came into his head. Rick composed most of the music 24,000 feet above America and Brazil while touring with the English Rock Ensemble.

It was his own personal journey into the unknown. 'I can't explain half of the record. Hence the title. But, basically it's a musical autobiography,' Rick told Chris Welch in *Melody Maker*. 'It's partly fictional and partly non-fictional, based on things everybody knows exists but they don't know why they exist. It deals with why life exists, what life there is under the sea, evolution, even flying saucers. Whether you believe in them or not, you can't discard 50,000 sightings a year.

'It concerns all the things we know about but can't explain. One of the few things that does grow, expand and develop is music. I took the human soul as my theme and explained it in musical terms. If a musician dies, then his soul, which is a musical soul, is reincarnated into another person. Everyone, when they were born, regardless of status, would be credited with a musical soul. Although the figure in my story is fictitious, it is a form of autobiography. It doesn't matter what walk of life you're born into, your environment and how you're brought up affects how your music soul is developed.

'So I split this album up into five parts, and none of the five shows what happens to this particular person but shows what could happen. It starts with a track called 'The Warning', where the child is born and the heart starts beating. It's the most important part of anybody's life when they don't have to make decisions for themselves, but the information given to them is what they base decisions on in the next few years. When you read eleven reviews of a concert and the first one says it was crap and the rest say it was great, then the first is the one that sticks with you.

'When kids are coming up to their teens they start asking questions and don't just accept what they're told, and one of the first questions is "Where do I come from?", and I don't just mean in the reproductive sense. Then it goes into a period of life which often destroys people that I've called 'The Spaceman', which is when people look too hard, and almost ruin their lives by dropping out of what they're good at, not necessarily music.

'Everyone goes through a period when they think to themselves; "What the hell I am I doing?" I defy anyone to say they haven't experienced aunts and uncles and grandmothers telling you: "I did that when I was your age. Now don't you go and do it." This is the period where the fictitious person is sitting by the fireside with his dog and his pipe thinking of all the things he's done wrong which is 'The Realization'. He realizes he's wrecked everything and it's too late to find his music soul and do anything with it. Then he looks at younger people coming up, possibly his own family and finds they won't listen to him, and it's too late. He's ruined himself - and there's nothing he can do. The final piece is called 'The Prisoner', who is punished on earth and then meets "the Maker", who tells him he is no use anywhere else, on other planes. The message is, if you do wrong, then you're left to wander the planes of space and time with nowhere to go.

'The last track, 'The Lost Cycle', deals in the huge gap in evolution. Somewhere along the line we've missed out on quite a few million years of development and I believe that there were civilizations on other planets a helluva lot further advanced than ours, who came exploring here. And the ideal place for them to live before they infiltrated was below the sea.' So that is where the triangle might come in. While he was writing this strange piece of music, Rick almost went insane. Classic madness is always lurking in the shadows of Wakeman's mind. A human can only cope with so much pressure before he cracks up. And that is something Rick knows only too well. During the American tour he allowed strange music to flood his brain. He wrote it all down in a jotter that went everywhere with him.

During the recording of the album at the Chateau de Herouville in France, where Elton John made his famous 'Honky Château' album - Rick found himself sitting on a wall in a tiny French village miles from the Chateau, crying his eyes out. 'I still don't know how I got there or why I was crying,' he said. 'It was as if my mind had blown a fuse.'

He had been working night and day. While the English Rock Ensemble were looning about in the specially hired jet, Rick found their noise was just a rumble in the background. 'Some of the writing was even done in the "little room",' said Rick. 'In fact, there are eight bars in the record which were written on the loo. They are heavily accented - they were done at a time of particular stress!'

Wakeman calls this astonishing way of composing - 'mind reaction'. He cannot explain how and why he is able to write in this way, he just accepts it and jots it down. 'I don't know anyone else in the world

who does this,' he says. 'Most people sit down at the piano and wait for inspiration. My method sounds weird, but to me it's perfectly natural. After all my years of training it's instinctive.

'The melody is in my head, I don't have to hum it or use an instrument to compose at. And yet the mind sound is never wrong when the group finally get to play it. It all comes out exactly as I'd imagined.'

Wakeman says his mind writing is as instinctive to him as some are playing the right shot at tennis. 'You don't think to yourself, "I must play a back-hand cross-court shot with plenty of top spin," you just do it naturally. It's the same with my music. I have an instinct and I go along with it.'

Rick's 'mind music' comes together in two volumes - a notebook for the words and ideas and a music manuscript book. He gives each phrase a letter and it may hang around for years before he decides it is what he wants. Then comes the difficult part - the orchestration, the emphasis of certain instruments and their skilful handling to produce the final balance. Not all his writing has been done at 24,000 feet, however; quite often it happens on stage, though not actually during concerts.

'I take the books with me during sound checks before shows. Even then new sounds and ideas come into my head,' he says. As well as the ever-present books he spends three hours a day in his studio at home making 'demos'. 'I've got a mixer, a tape deck and loads of keyboards. Sometimes a half-forgotten idea comes back and I think, "Oh that's good." And the following day it will probably come up again.'

Once a month Rick checks the tapes and files the best material on a separate reel. Although he has this almost supernatural writing ability, it was only when he was putting together words and music for 'No Earthly Connection' that he dared allow the phenomenon to take over.

'This was the first time I have been able to sit down for a consolidated period to write,' he said. 'I wrote a huge amount of music during the 'No Earthly Connection' record period, but sixty per cent of it had to be thrown out. I was determined to write down everything that came into my head. It was like the Thoughts of Chairman Wakeman. In fact, the band used to say, "Hello, Trotsky's off again!" But I had the last laugh. Any member of the band who insulted me suffered later because that provoked me to write an exceptionally difficult part for him to play.'

Singer Ashley Holt said, 'If I tied his shoe-laces together while he was writing that he'd say, "Here's a vocal part for you you won't forget in a hurry."' And the weather had a big influence too. 'He wrote the bad pieces when the plane went through turbulence,' said Ashley. 'It was a standing gag. He used to say, "If this plane drops out of the sky again I am going to write you the trickiest part you've ever had to play." And he did.' Rick said, 'They thought I'd changed my ways, when I sat there writing. Normally I was the chief loon, but I knew what I had to do this time.'

Wakeman may sound like a tyrant and in some ways he is. 'No one else tells me what or how to write, otherwise they wouldn't be my ideas,' he says. But he respects his musicians' abilities and opinions, and often allows them freedom to interpret his ideas in their own way.

'I tell them what I have in mind. The brass parts are written out, but on the rest everyone has a free hand. Nine times out of ten they come up with better ideas.' That's not surprising. Every musician who has worked with Rick is hand-picked after exhaustive auditions. They have to be good at their jobs - especially playing live - to cope with the highly sophisticated and varied time signatures in which he writes. And they must like curry! If there is dissent over a piece of music they would scrap it, he says everyone must be a hundred per cent happy with Wakeman's 'mind sound'. 'But we haven't had to scrap anything yet,' says Rick.

The subject matter of Wakeman's many top albums covers the wide range of music on which he has been brought up. 'The catalyst is the classical side, which produces what comes out,' he said. 'But I'm not trying to make rock fans interested in classical music. I've been lucky. My music's broken all rules with its classical influence and all the orchestras I've used - but it has sold.

'People enjoy it. That gives me satisfaction too. But you have to remember that music is big business. In theory you're writing for yourself Why? Because you want to. When music sells well, the record company wants you to stick to that style. But I develop new ideas which give them and myself heart attacks. Everyone has different views about what I should do - a rock keyboard, piano or classical album. Some think I should include lyrics, while others don't. I listen – and then ignore them. Of course, you get frustrating periods when people don't buy what you write and many musicians start writing false music, just to sell it. If the day comes when no one likes my albums there's nothing I can do. But I don't try to be different on purpose. That would be just as false, and I couldn't do anything I didn't believe in.'

But there's much more to Rick than being different - he is clever too. Very clever. English Rock Ensemble brass man Martyn Shields has played every type of music in the book. And he found Wakeman brought out the best in him. 'There's no doubt about it,' he said. 'This guy's a genius - a bloody genius.'

But it seems to be a mad genius that sometimes goes over the edge. It did in France. The period at the Château's recording studio was a period of great highs and lows for Rick. And while he was there the band got through 500 bottles of wine - a record for the Château. The snob sales-incentive from the vineyard is that you get your own name on the label if you order more than 600 bottles, and the banqueting table in the baronial hall was soon chequered with red bottles labelled "Vin Château de Herouville", like pawns in the game of getting stoned. The Château bustles with life. From the outside the Château can have changed little since it was first built more than 300 years ago, by none other than that great piano composer Chopin, as a *maison de rendezvous* for his lady love, the authoress, George Sands. And it is said to be haunted by him. Today the mansion rings to very different sounds of superstars like Cat Stevens, the first outsider to record there, *Jethro Tull*, John McLaughlin, the *Grateful Dead*, and, of course, Elton John.

Pink Floyd used the Château for their album 'Obscured by Clouds', and Elton made his big three, 'Don't Shoot Me', 'Yellow Brick Road', and 'Honky Château' there. After the work was complete, Mike Ledgerwood, A&M 's splendid Press Director, thought it would be a good idea to invite a party of Pressmen over for a preview of the album. I joined them in a luxury bus from London to the Château. We dubbed ourselves as the 'Horrorville Heroes' after a marathon journey there. We were greeted by Brian Lane who smiled uneasily through his black beard, as he gazed at the assembled throng. 'I'm sure you were all as surprised as I was to find Rick wasn't here, when we arrived tonight,' he said. Red faces all round - Rick had flown the roost and as our cheery charabanc to the Château travelled for nearly a whole day with wife Ros Wakeman among the travellers, Rick was headed for home..

But we did not know. So the rumours ran rampant. First it was thought Rick had gone for a spin in the country in his white Rolls. Then it seemed he had gone off in a rage after the band had switched his bedroom without telling him first. It was even feared he had gone to see Brentford beaten by Watford. With so many journalists around it seemed inevitable that a headline, 'Rock Star Rick is missing in Rolls', would appear somewhere. But the missing Rick re-appeared next day showing the ravages of

exhaustion. A nervous tic disturbed his face. His usually impressive hair looked bedraggled. His skin was red and his eyes betrayed weariness and wariness. He told journalist Harvey Lee of the *Watford Observer*; 'I've been working on the album for nine months now. I wrote it without ever playing any of it first. When I first heard the finished work in one go for the first time, it suddenly frightened me out of my mind. I thought to myself "Now I've got to do that on stage." The very thought of it had a strange effect on me. I can't quite explain. But it was why I suddenly left. I just got in the car and went home. And I didn't know what I was doing until I got back and people asked me what on earth I was doing when there were a party of Press people waiting at the Château to talk to me. I didn't even know what day it was.'

Lane arranged for a crop-spraying plane - the only one he could find - to fly Wakeman back from England for him to greet the Press. He did so with an embarrassed face, though after a few glasses of plonk, he was back to his normal self. And he told the strange tale of how a piece of marmalade nearly ruined the recording. He had accidentally flicked the orange jelly on to the master tape during a snack. 'Paul Tregurtha had to wash it, which took him hours. It could have been disastrous, because it was at the beginning of the tape. We would have had to ship the rhythm section back if he hadn't succeeded in salvaging that bit. About 300 feet of tape had to be washed with soap and water.' That was a small part of big worries and Rick also had to gee up his band to give their all. 'He would sometimes debag me and then send me to the mike with my trousers around my ankles to get me to relax,' said Ashley. 'He tries anything that will take out the tension at performing.' But sometimes tension is the winner and for a while a touch of madness takes over.

SIXTEEN
Dial-a-Laugh with Rick

To relax from the rigours of touring and writing, Rick took up a bizarre new hobby making a series of wacky telephone answering tapes. Now callers often prefer it when Rick's not available to answer the phone in person and they can listen to the zany recordings.

A recent dotty ditty for callers is sprinkled with references to wife Ros, au pair Viv, and characters from the long TV soap opera, *Crossroads*. I can't give Rick's number because the line is busy enough already, but this is the kind of thing that's giving his phone fans a giggle:

> . . . is the number of our 'phone.
> I'm afraid you've wasted four new
> pence,
> 'cos there's nobody at home.
> Ros is shopping down in Slough,
> The kids have done a bunk.
> Viv's out looking for the dogs.
> Rick's in bed drunk.
> Or he could be watching *Crossroads*,
> Which is more fun than reading.
> Amy Turtle might remember a line,
> Or Sandy get nicked for speeding.
> So kindly leave your name and number
> And we'll call you before long,
> Unless we owe you money,
> Then the ansafone stays on.

Rick told me: 'I've always wanted to be a comic and now I can - in the privacy of my own home.'

Even fellow rock stars such as Elton John have been ringing Rick's home for a few pence-worth of fun. But the answering machine is not always a laugh-a-minute. Like when Ros's car broke down and she tried to ring home for help. 'All I got was that damn machine talking about Amy Turtle,' complained Ros.

Rick's poetry might not be in the Wordsworth class, but it always gives him a belly laugh. Manager Brian Lane was the target for his verse in the programme of Rick's sell-out British tour with the *English Rock Ensemble*. It read:

> Brian Lane all the money is purging,
> With the Westminster Bank he is merging
> He says, 'Nothing for you'
> Like a typical Jew,
> He's as tight as an ant that's a virgin.

For some months Rick had been chopping and changing his line-up and for the 'No Earthly Connection' album he came up with what he considers his best *English Rock Ensemble* band. The personnel were: Ashley Holt, vocals; Roger Newell, bass guitar, bass pedals and vocals; John Dunsterville, acoustic and electric guitars and mandolin; Tony Fernandez, drums and percussion; Martyn Shields, trumpet, flugel horn, french horn and vocals; and Reg Brooks, trombone, bass trombone and vocals. John Dunsterville turned out to be the funniest man Rick had ever worked with, a true eccentric in the Keith Moon mould. Rick had discovered that this superb guitarist had retired from the music business and was running a perspex factory, in High Wycombe.

He also found out that John had his own full-size plastic camel in his back garden! He had bought it from a local art college and installed it, complete with open umbrella, so on balmy nights he could sit

under the moon and contemplate his navel.

Before 'No Earthly Connection' was made, the BBC completed a documentary in the series 'Success Story' on Rick's life. The TV film director, Alan Yentob, was a teetotaller before he discovered Rick. But Rick soon put a stop to that.

Wakeman said: 'When Alan came to make the film about me and my Wembley 'King Arthur' on ice concert, he didn't drink or smoke. By the time we were through with him he was doing twenty cigarettes a day and putting away as many pints as the rest of us. I think Alan had the idea that because we were serious musicians we would spend all our lives hunched over instruments or going for long walks in search of inspiration. We do work hard, but we found time to enjoy ourselves too, just drinking and fooling around like anybody else. Alan soon latched on to our life-style.'

The film was shown on BBC and Fred Randall once again showed his star quality. When asked by Yentob if Rick had a drink problem, he replied: 'Rick has no problem with drink. He just opens his mouth and down it goes.' A week after the screening of 'Success Story', Yentob's fifty-minute film of the three-hour Wembley show was shown at peak viewing time. Rick was already a big name around the world, but now at long last Britain was waking up to the phenomenal talents of the caped virtuoso.

It was ironic that Rick had toured all over the world, but never done a solo tour of his own country. So he decided to change all that - and the big audience break-through came when Rick and the band went out on the road in Britain, and then on to the Continent.

The concerts were like all his shows, a mixture of brilliant music and lots of giggles. Some journalists did not approve and one actually wrote: 'They probably have a rider in their contract which specifies that the *English Rock Ensemble's* dressing room must contain a communal bath into which they leap after a gig ends to hold farting contests deep into the night.'

But others liked the presentation. Of the first of three nights at the Hammersmith Odeon, Pauline McCloud in the *Daily Mirror* said:

> You could almost call it family entertainment. If it wasn't for the somewhat risqué jokes you could have taken the kids along. For I can't imagine any other concert with such a volume of rock, classical, choral and funfair music. Wakeman, long ago nicknamed king of the rock keyboard, lived up to his reputation. If he'd had longer arms he'd probably have added more keyboards to the stage. As it was he juggled his way between thirteen and a grand piano. But although the twenty-six-year-old musician is a mastermind of heavy rock, his absurd sense of humour filtered through. John Dunsterville played a beautiful serious piece of work on his Spanish guitar . . . until Wakeman moved in, Reg Dixon* style, to ruin it with a few minutes of fairground music. But their style of presentation came off. And hopefully in future, they will drag in a wider audience who would not normally bother with rock concerts. It was great to see a band who, though taking their work seriously, were able to laugh at themselves.

---

* Reginald Dixon MBE, ARCM, (16 October 1904 – 9 May 1985) was an English theatre organist.

He was best known as resident organist at the Tower Ballroom, Blackpool, where he played the Wurlitzer organ from 1930 until his retirement in 1970.

John Constable of the *Daily Telegraph* wrote:

> Judging by the enormously enjoyable and impeccably produced concert at the Hammersmith Odeon, economic stringency has done Rick Wakeman a great service. No longer do we have inflatable monsters fighting in lakes or medieval knights duelling on Wembley's ice. In their place this most accessible of 'superstar' musicians has substituted a more modest, but razor-sharp programme of his best compositions, performed with a sextet, the *English Rock Ensemble*, who have improved beyond all measure since last year's excesses.
>
> Wakeman never forgets his credo that entertainment is all. If the title extract from 'Journey to the Centre of the Earth' seemed too weighty an opening, the ribald spoken introductions, and the excellent John Dunsterville's self-parody of a classical guitar solo were the perfect levellers. Even the road crew were given a pantomime spot to open the second half. That spot was quite a hit, as each night the roadies mimed along with personalities from the audience a song which complained that since joining Wakeman they had 'laid nothing but a carpet'. It was a definite shift from Hollywood to Vaudeville ....

One of the shows, live at the Maltings, was shown on BBC 2's *Old Grey Whistle Test*. Even all the near-the-knuckle chat by Rick was allowed on this late evening screening.

While touring with the band, Rick took on his next record project – the soundtrack music for *White Rock*, a film on the triumphs and failures of competitors in the 1976 Winter Olympics. It was a tough project - for instance, how does a composer begin to convey a slalom contest in music? And how can the follow-up album bereft of visuals and plot, have any impact? Rick was only too aware that it is quite rare for film score LP.s to sell in great quantity. The moviemakers, Tony Maylam and Michael Samuelson, invited Rick to do the music after seeing his spectacular TV presentation of 'King Arthur' on ice from Wembley. Said director, Tony Maylam: 'Rick is no ordinary rock musician. His deep understanding of all aspects of music means he has been able to develop a further dimension to his work; a depth that is often lacking in the music of his contemporaries. His score for *White Rock* has contributed substantially to the film experience. It is a theatrical feature, in which moving pictures are not there merely to back up a rock score - but to blend with the music, to heighten the emotions, and to stimulate the mind.'

'I don't particularly like soundtrack albums myself,' Rick told Lorna Read of *Beat Instrumental*, 'but the album won't really be one. It'll just be based on the music I wrote for the film, with a lot added. I wouldn't say that soundtrack albums never sell - the albums from *2001* and *The Sting* sold on the strength of the film, even though people only knew the 'Thus Spake Zarathustra' theme and the first track of *The Sting*. I think that, providing it's all done completely again, re-recorded and remixed, it has a fair chance of selling.

'I've added many things which weren't in the film soundtrack, so it can stand up by itself.' Rick went on to describe the split-second timing needed in movie score work. 'I watched the completed film in a preview theatre with a timing sheet in my hand. The producer and director then decided what kind of music should go where,' Rick explained. 'Then it was my task to write music which was precisely timed to what was happening on the screen. In order to help the composer theyuse what are called "wipes", a line which comes across the screen after, say 33½ seconds or so behind or ahead.'

All the extra ideas that came to him while working on *White Rock* were put down with the help of Tony

Fernandez on drums and percussion. 'He's one of the most brilliant drummers in the rock world,' said Rick.

The film had a royal premiere with Princess Anne and Captain Mark Phillips at the opening night at the A.B.C. Theatre in Shaftesbury Avenue, London. Rick actually dressed up for the occasion and chatted with Princess Anne during the introductions.

The music was acclaimed by the critics. Nigel Andrews in the *Financial Times* said: 'Rick Wakeman's multi-track, multi-decibel rock music yowls and hums and throbs through *White Rock* . . . combined with Wakeman's shimmering, unearthly music, these sequences are extraordinary; pushing the technical possibilities of film to new limits.'

While Arthur Thirkell in the *Daily Mirror* said: 'Rock musician Rick Wakeman's score, using keyboard, percussion and choral themes, heightens the drama in a superb documentary.'

Alan Brien in the *Sunday Times* said: 'There is an electrifying, multi-sound score by Rick Wakeman and a gratifying real, but also impressively gutsy, guide in James Coburn who actually attempts some of the Olympian ordeals in the way we like to think we would.'

The critic from *Sounds* magazine Phillis Stein said:

> *White Rock* has Rick Wakeman writing the soundtrack to a highly individual view of the 1976 Winter Olympics in Innsbruck, Austria, which is fronted by James Coburn.
>
> . . . I rather feared for Wakeman's soundtrack, particularly as Rick is not best known for using one keyboard where eighteen will do.
>
> But to my surprise Wakeman manages to keep a better sense of proportion than everyone else around him. His score manages to get something of the grace and beauty of the skiers, tobogganers and downhill racers combined with the fierce competitive spirit that drives them to the limit of their ability and often beyond as we see with shots of beaten goalies, fallen skiers and jumpers - all starkly contrasted with the smiles of the victor.
>
> I'm no sports fanatic, but despite Coburn's extravagances, I found myself drawn into the dedicated and painfully single-minded world of the Olympic athlete via Wakeman's music and some superb colour photography and almost unbelievable filming angles (particularly on the ski-jumping and downhill racing).

The music for *White Rock* took five weeks to record at C.T.S. and Advision Studios in London. Every track was written, produced and performed by Rick. Over ninety hours was spent mixing the twenty-four instrument and vocal tracks down to the film stereo soundtrack. The final blend of music and sounds is unique - it surely must be one of the most original and powerful cinema scores ever written. Besides the percussion contribution of Tony Fernandez, there was also vocal assistance from the choir of St Paul's Cathedral, London. '*White Rock*' went into the British charts at number fourteen. At last Rick and the band were receiving the acclaim he had striven for years - for lyrics and music.

Things could only get better. Or could they?

SEVENTEEN
Whisky on the Rocks

It should have been the happiest moment of Rick's life. He had just taken his *English Rock Ensemble* on a sell-out tour of twenty-six British cities and then gone to a similar number of European venues. He had appeared on the prestigious BBC television *Old Grey Whistle Test* show - they had screened the whole of a live concert - and the Press had really begun to fete his vast talent as a performer and composer.

Night after night Wakeman, in his bejewelled cape, had received standing ovations for spectacular presentations of excerpts from 'Six Wives', 'Journey', 'Arthur' and 'No Earthly Connection'.

Recalled Rick: 'The whole tour had been a smash. After performing so much in North and South America as well as Japan, Australia and New Zealand, it was a knockout to be able to play in Europe again.'

But despite the acclaim Rick came home to his Buckinghamshire mansion to find he could not stop drinking. And the whisky nearly drove him on the rocks.

'For a whole week I stayed in the "Brahms and Liszt Bar" at the top of my house and drank bottle after bottle of Scotch. I didn't answer the door or phone for a whole week,' he said. 'Ros had taken the kids to our farm in Devon so I had no interruptions during my crazy bender.'

So what was the problem? What on earth had caused the life and soul of every party to nearly kill himself with booze? 'A small matter of £350,000 which I had to find in a matter of weeks,' he said.

After all the work Rick and his band had put into the European tour, they should have expected a tidy profit, so it was like a punch in the face from Muhammad Ali when Rick's London accountant David Moss told him the grim news: 'Rick, I'm afraid the profit from the is tour is nowhere like it should have been. In fact it's minimal, while your expenses have been absolutely phenomenal. And besides that you've got a lot of urgent matters to attend to.'

In fact, Moss left Rick in no doubts that if £350,000 was not raised very quickly, he would be on the rocks.

'It wasn't an all tax problem, because I always settled that in time, but it mainly concerned my other interests,' said Rick. The bad news about the companies was certainly a nasty shock after seven weeks' hard, gratifying labour on the road with the band and the road crew, who always went on ahead in the articulated lorry carrying Wakeman's £80,000 battery of keyboards.

'I decided to take a long hard look at my financial commitments and see where I could make cuts,' he said. 'The first thing I had to do was to sell my beloved Rolls-Royces. I got rid of seven in a matter of days. It was heartbreaking. That just left me with the Silver Cloud Three with my personal number plate - RW 100. I then had to call in the Receiver for the Fragile Carriage Company. Another sad moment.'

Rick says this shock news again caused his mind to become unhinged for a time. 'In a twelve-month period I had been on the edge of complete insanity on four occasions. But this was the worst. I became completely paranoiac and was convinced that everyone was plotting to destroy me.

'I even turned against my old friend and manager Brian Lane. I phoned him in Los Angeles, where he was staying with *Yes*, and told him of my problems. He said, "Rick, it's no good talking on the phone, get the first plane here and let's sort this out." He told me that I could see the people at the A&M Hollywood office at the same time.'

So Wakeman headed for the West Coast of America and had a real heart-to-heart with Lane. The shrewd manager had been through many crises with Rick, and took this one as nothing unusual. 'After talking to Brian for ages I went to the A&M office and was angry to find that most of the people I wanted to see were away. I was so mad I just boiled over and took it out on those who were there. I had a big row and told them that I felt - wrongly, as it later turned out - that they had not properly promoted my last American tour. I just lashed out at the time. I'd never before rowed with anyone at A&M

'Anyway, I talked and talked with Brian and sometimes it got a little heated. We both knew each other well enough to gloss over the rows, but he could see this time I was really deadly serious. We talked of ways in which I could raise cash without completely crippling myself with loans. We knew I was due big royalties for projects I had already completed – like '*White Rock*' - but the money was not due for another four months. That was no good, I needed it straight away.

'I was so angry with Brian that I decided there and then to break from him and get new management in England. Brian and I didn't have a contract so it could be done quickly and without too much legal wrangling.

'I flew home via Washington so that I could ride in Concorde - I thought that might cheer me up, but it didn't – and then I went to see my London lawyer and accountant. They said I had to take really urgent measures to cut my expenses.

'It was then I saw that I had to take the heartrending decision to disband the English Rock Ensemble before the barrel completely ran out and we all went under. But each member was a personal mate – not just someone I worked with professionally. We had lived in each other's pockets for so long and shared so much fun touring the world. But I knew I had to do it because I just didn't have the money to keep paying them.

'I knew the decision would cause many problems for some of the lads and that some would have to go on the dole, a humiliating prospect after playing in front of thousands of fans around the world. I knew others, however, would have no bother at all in getting new work, because they had been around so long and had built up such reputations. That is just how it has worked out. But there was just no more money to pay them.'

So Rick summoned the lads to the upper room of their regular social centre, a pub in High Wycombe, close to Complex Seven, where Rick had housed many of his commercial projects.

'We had a few uneasy drinks in the downstairs bar and then tramped up the stairs,' recalled Rick. 'There was a stunned silence as I told them the situation. I felt their hurt as I talked, and found it a terrible task. I suppose if we had all had lots of rows and didn't get on, it would have been easier, but that was not so. I found telling them the most difficult thing I have ever had to do. I shook hands with them all - Ashley, Budgie, Martyn, Reg, Tony and John - and then stumbled out of the room.'

Their last dates together were on 13th August 1976, where they headlined a festival at Bilzen, Belgium.

Rick told me: 'I was very sad to break up the band as they had become a very tight unit - I mean that musically . . . But I must add that they had quite a few opportunities to do things on their own, but they didn't. That might have been an insurance policy for them.'

Rick also decided to press ahead with the split with Brian Lane, but no public announcement was made until Lane arrived back in London. 'I felt we should both be in Britain when the announcement was made,' said Rick.

But then came the shattering increase to eighteen per cent - in Britain's Bank Rate. 'That completely knocked the bottom out of everything,' Rick went on. 'Suddenly financial problems that were due to come up in a month's time had already happened, as it were.

'I called an emergency meeting with Derek Green, British boss of A&M , and told him all about my problems. I complained that I thought the American part of the company hadn't properly promoted my last American tour, and generally had a good moan. Derek listened with great sympathy and then made a marvellous gesture. He said he would try and get to see Jerry Moss, the 'M' in A&M and work out a formula to rescue me from financial disaster. Moss was in the South of France so he had a long way to go.

'When Derek Green got back, he told me that A&M would settle all my financial problems for me by paying royalties ahead of time and things like that. It was a great gesture.

'Brian then came back from Los Angeles and with me in a more relaxed mood, we decided to carry on together.'

Ironically, offers of work suddenly began to flood in for Rick. Film companies wanted him to do scores for movies, and TV companies wanted theme tunes for programmes. Rick found the prospect very tempting.

'It would have been big money and certainly interesting to do, but I began to think that my life was rock 'n' roll. That was my bread and butter, while films were just the jam.'

So Lane came up with what seemed a sensible suggestion – of forming a band with musicians who were already self-sufficient.

'By pure coincidence Bill Bruford, my ex-colleague from *Yes*, and John Wetton, the ex-*Uriah Heep* bass player, were then thinking along the same lines,' said Rick.

'We had a private meeting and decided to start rehearsing. We went to my rehearsal studios at Complex Seven and worked hard for six weeks. We were just getting it all together when the story leaked out in the *Melody Maker*. There slap on the front page was the story of the new "super-group".'

The story dated 16th October 1976, read:

> Wakeman, Bruford and Wetton - that's the line-up of a new supergroup being planned as rivals to *Emerson, Lake and Palmer*.
>
> Since the break-up of the *English Rock Ensemble* earlier this year, Rick Wakeman has concentrated on studio work. But now he is teaming up with an old colleague from *Yes*, drummer Bill Bruford, and the ex-*Uriah Heep* bass player, John Wetton.
>
> Details of the new band are being kept under wraps.
>
> Bruford has been on the road during most of this year, first with *Genesis* and now with *National Health*. John Wetton, who has been a member of both Family and *King Crimson*, quit *Uriah Heep* this summer and is currently working on Bryan Ferry's solo album.
>
> Wakeman, meanwhile, releases a new album. Called '*White Rock*', the album features the soundtrack music for a film made at the Winter Olympics.

The story caused the rehearsing trio insurmountable problems. 'We were really in a spot because we all had different recording companies, music publishers, PRs and managers,' said Rick. 'Each one wanted the best deal for his artiste and it got very silly in the end. We would spend the first four hours of each rehearsal on the phone, trying to agree deals with various people, but we couldn't agree on anything. It was like a bad dream, especially after all those weeks of rehearsal. We didn't even agree on a name, though it could well have been British Legion in the end.'

Rick's luck finally began to change when Alex Scott, Brian Lane's partner, flew into London and renewed the invitation to Rick to again become a session musician - with *Yes*. To reinforce the plan, Brian made a special journey from Switzerland, where *Yes* were about to start recording, to try and persuade Rick to fly back with him to 'meet the boys and talk the whole thing over'.

Said Rick: 'I agreed to meet with the group. I must admit that I was full of apprehension because I didn't know how they would receive me after some of the nasty things I'd said about them in the past.

'And I was also afraid of losing my identity by just becoming a member of *Yes*. But to my surprise I found that they had changed drastically and each had become an individual. I think that the problem before was that I was the only one in *Yes* making solo albums and this had given me outside interest. The rest of the group found all their interests within *Yes*.

'But now they told me they had all made their own solo albums and had become individuals who got together to make up *Yes*. The health-food kick had also changed, and I found the only true vegetarian left was Steve Howe. I found to my utter surprise that they all now drank alcohol. And we began relating to each other for the first time. I think we had all grown up and become much more mature. Maybe I had to grow up more than them.

'They said before I made up my mind to play on the sessions I could listen to the demo recording they had done. It was amazing, much more like the old *Yes*. I said I could definitely play on this.

'Atlantic Records threw a party that night and during it the lads put it to me that they wanted me not just to play on the album, but also to re-join the group full-time. They said they wanted me to go on tour with them and play on the next album.

'As we talked together it suddenly dawned on me that the reason that I left *Yes* in the first place was because I had been living two lives, while they only had one - the group. They couldn't understand why I had so many outside interests; I couldn't understand why the group meant so much to them and now suddenly *Yes* meant so much more to me than ever before. In their field, *Yes* are untouchable. I feel proud to have re-joined them.

'Especially after having been so close to the edge. My return has been made that much sweeter by our first album back together, 'Going For The One', reached number one in every English chart.'

A near miss - Rick recovers from a car accident in Switzerland, January 1977

EIGHTEEN

Wakeman on Wakeman

One of the great paradoxes of Rick Wakeman's strange life is that although he is respected by millions around the world, he's never sure who his real friends are. He realized this when an American businessman said to him; 'I feel really sorry for you Rick, you haven't got a friend in the world. You don't know who your friends are and aren't.'

Said Rick: 'In a strange way that is perfectly true. People like to be involved with someone successful, and if you've got the trappings of success, like a big house and a Rolls-Royce, they want to be with you, to hang on. But the difficulty is to sort out those who really want to know you because you're Rick Wakeman, nice guy, and those who want you because you're Rick Wakeman, successful rock star, from whom they might get certain benefits from hanging around. They are the sort who would drop you if it all fell apart. I often don't know who's who in this respect.

'My friendships, if you can call them that, are more communal than individual. I would call all those who were in the English Rock Ensemble friends, to the extent that I could confide in them. But even that friendship went sour inasmuch as I had to sack them all in the end for financial reasons. And that was the hardest task I've ever had to do. I always bore in mind with them that although we had lots of fun, it was still an employer-employee relationship. It made me very lonely at times. You see, you cannot afford to make a mistake. My philosophy then was that if they stepped out of line they would have got the sack, though as I've already said, that wasn't why I closed down the band.'

Rick added: 'I find the people I feel I can trust most are those I don't really know. Complete strangers. I often find I can really chat to them.

'A strange thing in my world, which I find quite a burden, is the fact that I'm never supposed to change my mind. For instance, the ordinary man in the street can constantly change his ideas. He can say brown is his favourite colour one day and pink the next. I'm supposed to say it is the same all the time.'

I asked Rick if he got frustrated when people did not understand him and his music. 'I don't think anybody understands me,' he admitted. 'To be honest, I don't think I understand myself. Some people say I am

OPPOSITE: Rick with the author, who studied him for three years before writing this book

on the borderline of madness and genius. Well, I am certainly on the edge of madness. I often loon about as a safety valve. There are definitely two sides to me - and they are both excessive. I'm often asked why a lunatic like me writes such sensitive, serious music. I've never really been able to explain what makes me do it. I know in my mind exactly what it's all about. But there aren't words in the English dictionary to describe how I feel. But that's not the hardest problem. That is the emotional side. Sometimes, for instance, I'm away when a family needs to be a family. Silly little things happen or like when our donkey in Devon died, and I was in America. That may sound unimportant, but it was an upsetting time for all of us.

'Even more important was the fact that both my children were born while I was touring so I didn't see them for some time. If I had a wife who was very demanding and wanted to go everywhere with me, it couldn't work. Luckily Ros grew up with it gradually, though I know I she doesn't like it at times. But equally she knows that if I quit it all and lived at home, that would be even more damaging, because I couldn't do it. I'd go completely mad.

'I must admit my life is a constant conflict. I love my family deeply, but I also love music. Theoretically the two don't mix, they are time bombs with two fuses, but somehow they haven't yet blown up in my case. I know that I must somehow stick to my frenetic life and steam away. Recently, for instance, I've been in Switzerland with *Yes*, and I've only been home twice, for Adam's and Oliver's (below) birthdays. Both were flying visits. I also miss not being able to see Brentford play.'

Rick says he is closer to his mother and father since he married than he ever was when he lived with them. And he discovered how strong the bond was just before he left one day for a tour with the *English Rock Ensemble*, when his mother announced his dad was also suffering from a heart problem.

'My mum seems really hard - but in fact she's the best Samaritan in the world and she'd do anything to help anybody. And she usually does it with such calm. But that day I saw her cry for the first I time. "Your dad's really ill," she told me. "But he's a stubborn man and refuses to go to a doctor."

'I thought, "You stubborn old sod. I'll get you to go." And so I phoned Brian at his house, even though it was about 1am. I knew he knew an incredible doctor in London who had his own clinic. Brian said he would do all he could.

'Then I phoned up dad and threatened to break off all diplomatic relations unless he went. He agreed. The doctor examined him and said he was very ill. He diagnosed dad had heart trouble, kidney trouble and liver trouble. And he said his heart was about three times the size it should have been and he had giant stones in his kidney. If dad had gone two weeks later he would have been brought in in a wooden box.

'They put dad in a nursing home in Holland Park, London, and managed to save his life. He's much better now. My next crusade is to make him retire. I know he likes his work, but for his health's sake he's got to retire - though I'm a fine one to say this! He loves Devon, where my farm is, so I'm trying to get him to go and live in that area.

'I have a deep regard for both my mum and dad. The trouble with the Wakemans is we're all terribly stubborn people. And not only are we stubborn but we keep a lot of things to ourselves and don't talk about them. Also, we often like to be on our own with nobody else about. My dad's a bit like that. My mum's stubborn in the nicest sense of the word and a lovely old fusspot. I do things deliberately to annoy her. I own up to that. For instance even now she says, "Are you going to wash your hair?" and I'll say, "No", knowing it will upset her. "I'm not planning to wash it for at least three weeks," I will say. She looks horrified at me. Ros has a go at me because I really get mum going. I can't help it, it's just my nature!'

What is Rick's relationship with music critics who slate him? 'Well, they used to worry me, but now quite honestly I really I don't care at all, because if the people who buy the records enjoy them and people who listen to the music enjoy it, then that is really all that matters. Unfortunately, there are too many journalists around nowadays who think their name at the bottom of the little article they have written is more important than the music they are writing about. The same goes for films as well, but the right thing is what Ken Russell once said to me: "When they take a page to slag you off, then you know you are on the way."'

How does Rick now get on with his manager Brian Lane? 'I think the world of Brian in one way and I think he's a "schmock" in another. I interfere with what he does sometimes and he does the same with me. But as far as managers go, he is the best around today. He's a good wheeler-dealer. He understands the music business very well. He's been in it a long time at all levels, and he knows what it's all about. I really know very little about the music management side of things. I try to keep out of it as much as I can. But at times I'm forced in, and that's when Brian and I row. I tell him what to do and he tells me: "Go forth and multiply", or words to that effect! Mind you, I tell him the same when he tries to talk to me about music. We row constantly. He often thinks my business ideas are ludicrous and I think the same about his music ideas. Brian doesn't understand my music at all. He's tone deaf and has got cloth

Wedding anniversary party

ears, but he knows whether it's good or not and whether he can sell it. And if anybody can sell something, Brian can. That's where he's excellent. I think our friction makes for the perfect business relationship and friendship. We have a really terrible row and then go out for a meal or a drink and we are mates again. At the time the shouting is serious, but we can then cut off. Sometimes I feel like saying, "I'm going to get another manager," but I realize there isn't anybody around as good as he is. You can have all the music talent in the world, but if you're not handled properly, it can all be wasted. It's doubtful if another Brian Lane will exist.'

Rick is never embarrassed to talk to fans and never gives the usual 'You can't touch me' superstar brush-off. In fact, I've seen him minutes before a big concert having a quiet drink in a pub and chatting to people.

'The funniest guy that ever came up and spoke to me was amazing. And I was bowled over with laughter when I realized it was a gag. He told me: "I went to your concert at Wembley, man." "Oh, did you like it?" "No, I thought it was the worst thing I've ever seen in my life." "Pardon?" "It was awful." "What didn't you like?" "What do you mean?" "Well, tell me what bit you didn't like and I'll tell you why I did it." He laughed and said, "I only came up to see if you would hit us or something. We couldn't get tickets for Wembley anyway."

'I am always happy to talk to anybody, though sometimes they butt in at the most inopportune times. You can often size up people who come up for an autograph and realize they are more embarrassed than you. Most people say it's for their daughter, but when you ask what their daughter's name is, they say: "Don't bother to put it to anyone, just give us your autograph."

'I get on really well with the big names in the business, though I'm not star-struck at all. I've never had a rock idol that I've wanted to meet madly, though I would I like to meet Edward Heath because he impresses me both as a person and a musician. And we both love organs.

'What does bore me about many musicians is that their conversation often begins and ends with music. And quite often that's the last thing I want to talk about. I'd much rather talk about cars, football or horse racing.'

Although he often appears the original heathen, Rick has a genuine interest in Christianity.

'I once took a Scripture exam at Sunday School and ended up with a ninety-eight per cent pass, winning an all-England Scripture prize,' he remembers, adding with a smile: 'It was such a shock to the people at church, they jokingly accused me of bribing the examiners.'

Rick occasionally reads his Bible and prays. 'I find prayer, especially, very helpful,' he says. 'I pray about weird things. For example, I met a young girl and boy on a tour of Holland. They were badly hooked on hard drugs and, to be honest, close to death. I prayed hard for them, as I did for a young junkie I met in Piccadilly Circus, who was writing his last will and testament. I have prayed for guidance for myself when I have been in tight positions and, believe you me, when you're a musician you're vulnerable to meet every problem in the world - from starvation to insanity.'

I asked Rick about his strong views against drugs. 'Drugs upset me,' he said. 'The drug scene, however, isn't new. Charlie Parker took drugs in the forties. It's the Press, in my opinion, who have caused this enormous rise in drug taking with their constant publicity. They arouse people's interest in them. 'Would I take drugs under any circumstances? Well, when I was in Holland with the *Strawbs* and broke my foot I refused a pain-killing injection because of my fear of needles - does that answer your question? Since then, however, I have taken pills for my heart trouble, though I have stopped them now.'

Rick has an unusual suggestion which he thinks might cut down drug abuse in Britain. 'I think we should show the kind of television programme they do in America. There, they have a junkie on each night who has only, say, a week to live, and he tells of his last week alive. 'I've seen people on trips, stoned out of their heads. People I know personally have died through drugs. But it's hard to stop addicts once they're on, and I think prevention is better than cure. I've managed to stop two people going on drugs. If we get the facts over to the twelve-year-olds now, then we may be able to wipe out the present disastrous situation.'

And what advice would Rick give to a young talented musician who had a safe job but wanted to give it up to break into the professional music scene?

'Let's put it this way,' said Rick. 'Ninety per cent of today's musicians are broke. But, if the opportunity arrives for a young, talented musician to become professional and he's willing to rough it and be trodden on, ridiculed, hurt, abused and come out smiling, then I would admire him and welcome him to the throngs of maniacs like myself. It's very tough. I've cried myself to sleep on more than one occasion, and also thought of jacking it all in. If I wasn't convinced that God had put me here to see what I have seen and do what I have done, I certainly would have taken a safe job.'

Looking back on his strenuous session days, Rick has some hard words for some session men. 'You get plenty of them who have said, "Right, it's time for our tea break. It's now two minutes to nine and you realize that if it goes on after then we'll be charging up for a half session, according to clause 3, part B or whatever it is, of the Musicians Union code." This to me is dreadful. These guys never seem to identify with the artiste or band they are working for on the session, and they don't make many friends. Mind you, they make a lot of money. They're not musicians in my opinion, they're just mechanical beings who turn up, do their bit, collect their money and go home. Thank heaven most session musicians enjoy their music before union rules.

'I used to get embarrassed sometimes when a session went over time and I got extra pay . . . I used to feel I was partly responsible for things not working it out on schedule.'

But what if his career had gone in a different direction? Does he think he would have made it as a classical pianist? 'You've got to remember that everyone who undertakes classical instruction has thoughts about becoming a concert pianist at the beginning, but very few make the grade. Those who do have to be extremely dedicated and generally concentrate on one composer - you know, they're the king when it comes to that composer's music. I've always liked to dabble with so many things and I could never have made it on that basis.

'At present, rock fans are beginning to listen to classical material, but the classical people just don't realize that rock has an important contribution to make, which is a great pity. My favourite classical composers are Mozart for his melodies and Rachmaninov for his orchestration. I'm a bit of a Mozart freak, but I don't like everything he did. You can like a style of somebody's work, but it doesn't mean you've got to like everything they do. I think Mozart has directed my composing as far as my melodies go, and Rachmaninov has inspired me when I orchestrate. My piano playing is very Mozart, but I think I've basically been influenced by everybody's music I've played, which is every classical composer in the book.

'I don't think I identify with any composer of those days for they were from a totally different age. They wrote and worked differently. And music then was treated in a totally different way. They didn't have the problems I have and I don't have the problems they had.

'For instance, more often than not, they were working for a court and they'd be told what to write. The composer would be summoned before the Count and told: "I want a mazurka for tomorrow night." Now the guy might not feel like writing a mazurka, but he had to write one.

'Everything they wrote then was classed as very serious, but the problem is I have to convince certain people who either think my music is incredibly highbrow or is just a load of rubbish, that it is deadly serious and merits a listen. I don't put together classical and rock in my music as a gimmick, it is there because it's the only way I know how to write. You compose according to your upbringing. I suppose the catalyst has always been the classical side of things, but I just throw everything in together and see what comes out. There is no other way I know how to write, so I'm not particularly trying to do something clever, it's just the only way I know how to do it. I'm not trying to make rock fans interested in classical music. Whether you like it or not, music is big business. Theoretically you are writing for yourself, but really you are under great pressure from other people to write to what is a winning format.

But I won't do that, I break all the rules in my styles and this gives those around me heart attacks. But if people are enjoying my music, that is really satisfying to me. I've never written anything I've not believed in and I'll stand by it now, even though some of it was slated at the time.

'Everyone has different ideas on what my next album should be, so I listen to them, and then politely ignore what they say and just carry on with what I know how to do best. I say, "Look, I only know one way of doing things, and I'm going to carry on doing it." If the day comes when people don't like what I'm doing, there's not really much I can do about it.

'I know my albums are very different to other people's, but I don't do that consciously. Because if you do that, you are producing false music. Music is one of the strangest things in the world. It comes from nowhere. You sit down at a piano and you can't say it starts on the first note because there are only twelve notes you can start on and yet there are millions of tunes around. I can't really understand how themes start up in my head, but they do. Music is one of life's great mysteries.

'I hate writing to formula, to a time and length, though I can do it. I've written pieces of music that are only twenty-five seconds long, like the little choir bits on 'Arthur'. I find that a piece of music just grows and grows automatically and it finishes at a natural point. If you let it flow, it ends naturally. I'd hate to write little pop tunes. They are usually so predictable.

'One of my ambitions is to send all pop musicians to the Royal College of Music for a week and watch most die the death, and send all the classical students on the road with a band for a week and watch them do the same. Those who manage to survive both are the musicians worth talking about.'

Is Rick glad he continued with his piano lessons? 'Yes certainly, though in my teens it was difficult. I think you get periods where other things start happening, especially around the beginning of the teens, thirteen and fourteen, when your mates are out playing football or going out with girls and discovering other delights in the world. I was stuck in practising at that time. Right up to twelve or thirteen, nearly every other kid is playing the piano or learning to make cat noises on the violin or something, but suddenly if you can get over that period - my parents and my music teacher helped by encouraging me - when you come to about fifteen or sixteen you realize that there are only a handful of you left playing the piano, because everybody else has dropped out.

'There are loads of people I have talked to who say; "I used to learn to play the piano, but I packed up when I was eleven or twelve, I wish I hadn't." It's the age-old story, hundreds of people do it.'

What exactly does his classical training add to his music? 'It's helped me technique-wise and obviously in orchestration and understanding how to put parts together, how to orchestrate different colourings that classical music has. Any form of colour is the one thing that modern pop music - for want of a better word - lacks dreadfully. That's why I got involved in all the other forms of keyboards, to add all those different effects, different colourings. So when I get an idea in my head I can play it through my classical training.'

What kind of themes has Rick used or borrowed? 'I've borrowed a couple, not for any specific reasons but because they suited what I was writing. In 'Journey to the Centre of the Earth', for instance, there was one part in one translation of the book when the raft was being shot through the volcano and up the shaft, and at one point the water which was being pushed up by the eruption stopped which meant that the raft lay dormant and everything had stopped. The book described it as if they were in a huge hall with the King of the Mountain, and it was obvious I had to fill up a part to illustrate that and I used Grieg's 'Hall of the Mountain King'.'

Why is Rick so interested in spectacular forms of music? 'With the instruments I've got I can do lots and lots of things. I have instruments that can create string sounds, or violin sounds, cello sounds, trumpet sounds, choral sounds, but they all lack the human element. I can do things on them for example that the human being can't do. I could play some trumpet lifts that sound almost like a trumpet, that no human trumpet player could possibly play. On the other hand the trumpet player can do lots and lots of things that I can't do on an instrument, so when I write the pieces of music, I hear the sounds that I want in my head. And if I can do them and the sounds are right for the synthesized orchestrations that I want to do, then I don't use any other instruments.'

One of the most interesting people Rick has met was Dr Robert A. Moog, the father of the modern music synthesizer. And Wakeman has played a major part in exploiting the Moog as a vehicle for developing rock music.

'Our meeting was unexpected,' said Rick. 'It was while I was in Buffalo with *Yes*. We booked into the local Holiday Inn and I went to the restaurant. I was sitting there minding my own business when suddenly two men walked up to me and sat down each side of me. I thought they were from the Mafia - and they just looked at me and said: "We've been sent down to see you." I was getting really worried until they told me they were from the Moog Corporation. All they wanted to know was whether I was happy with the instrument and whether I had any criticisms or ideas for improvements to its design.

'I was impressed with the request. That's what makes Moog so different from a lot of other companies. Moog have constant design improvement programmes and they go to the users - the musicians - to get their ideas. How many other companies do that?

'Anyway, it turned out that the next evening's gig was only fifty miles from where Moog have their headquarters, so I stopped off on the way and got a chance to meet the great Dr Moog. He was a fantastic character, really great - just like everyone's idea of the absent-minded professor, a lovely geezer who's revolutionized keyboards. And I was just as enthralled by the things he had to show me, and the new ideas they're working on. I was particularly impressed with a form memory cell they've designed. It's like a sequencer, in that it remembers a series of notes or programme instructions. But the memory cell has a far greater capacity.'

Rick is a great believer in knowing as much as possible about the weird and wonderful electronic instruments he wrestles with on stage.

'I always fully investigate and try out an instrument before taking it out on the road. For instance, it takes me only a couple of days to really understand all the little quirks and faults of an electric piano. I usually have it at home and play around with it. Then I make a list of things I want altered and it goes down to my factory for Toby Errington, my electronics expert, to modify. Then it comes back to my house for more trials. If I'm satisfied, it goes out on the road with me.

'Obviously a Moog is far more complex and it can be anything up to a year before it goes out with me. I have to know everything possible about what does what before I even ask Toby to do the modifications I want. These Moogs are a bit like flying an aircraft, and there are a lot of built-in safety measures, so that if something goes wrong on stage you can always use an alternative method and go over to another bank of instruments.

'You can always tell when you are on the road to success because you don't have to get in contact with the manufacturers any more - they start coming to you and sending you new things. So you often come across instruments you would never normally hear about. Salesmen usually come and see me with their

"Rick's one of the new breed of computer men, he was on the Old Grey Whistle Test last week."

new instruments, though some also send leaflets and all the gumph. Usually I get about forty instruments sent to me each year and I analyse all of them if I can. If they are American and I'm not there, I get a very good friend of mine, Greg Hockman, who used to be Bob Moog's right-hand man, to check them out for me.

'I couldn't fix one of my instruments if it broke down, but I usually know exactly what is wrong. I can grasp sounds and know what makes what sounds. I can point out to Toby on a wiring diagram what is wrong, but I can't actually repair it. That's why I need a guy on the road with me all the time. But it is vital for me to understand all my instruments. For, if say half-an-hour before a concert, I shouted to him and said: "Toby, my Moog's conked out. I don't know what's wrong with it" - that's like taking your car to a garage and saying, "I don't know what's wrong, all I know is it isn't right." You have got to be able to say to Toby, "The modulation pitch wheel is jammed. I need a new one." That could be fixed in five minutes and means you can still use the instrument for the concert.'

In an interview with John Boulton in *Sounds*, Rick gave lots of good advice to the electronic keyboard freaks and explained why he is master of his craft. 'Most people know about Moogs and the basic electric pianos,' he said, 'but it's the adaptations you can have done to instruments and things to use with them, to change the sound, I find interesting.' Incidentally, all of Rick's keyboards have been rebuilt by Systems and Technology in Kalamazoo, USA.

The *Sounds* interview added: 'I would advise anyone going to buy instruments to look very closely at what sort of pedals they can put with them, because the days of playing an instrument with straight sounds are really gone. This is because of all the clever things you can do in the studio, for when you go out on the road people expect to hear them, so you have to have the same sort of equipment.

'Moogs are basically straightforward. There are so many different sorts of synthesizer that you can't really recommend one against another, as it's purely a matter of personal taste. It's virtually why one person chooses to drive a Vauxhall and another a Ford. There are now some polyphonic synthesizers on the market, but I'm not sold on them yet. I own a Moog polyphonic, but I'm very biased towards Moog but I don't think it compares as well to all their other products, the modified Moogs, the Synthi, the Mini Moog and the P1, P2, P3 and the C series. To me professionally, they are really good instruments that you can rely on. I know that the polyphonic Moog has the same components basically, but for some unknown reason it's not quite right yet.

'Ironically, one way you can find this out is by just multi-tracking Moogs. If you track say twenty-four Moogs, you end up not with the sound of twenty-four Moogs but something like a church organ sound with all the stops out. That's, of course, if you have the same setting and the same sound. If you have different sounds, then that would be great, but they don't actually work like that and I think that until they do, rather than have a single manual Moog that was polyphonic, I would rather see a double manual or a three manual Moog and that I feel would be more advantageous.

'Concerning other instruments that aren't that common, there is one that my company makes called the Birontron, which is an instrument that re-creates orchestral sounds very reliably, with very light action, touch. and no delay. The other thing I like is the RMI computer piano. It's bloody expensive, about $7,000 to buy, but it really is incredible. You've got computer cards and you can feed all these cards into the card reader, so you have four different readings of whatever instrument you want. So let's say you do alto sax, a bell, a sine wave and flute. You have the four and combinations of the four and add in other little novelties that they've built into the instrument, and it contains twelve memory banks so it will retain anything that you ask it to do, providing that you play it.'

What about the amplification side?

'Well I either use Crowns or SAE's and a Soundcraft mixer, everything gets fed into them, and there are three feeds, one to the monitors, one to the desk and then one to me, that goes into the SAE's or the Crowns, and don't ask me what these speakers are, but we developed the "trouser flapper", which really is something else, and it's in a not particularly large cabinet that I have down in front of me and with two horns on the top. Exactly what the speaker is I couldn't tell you, but it ain't "'alf bloody good".'

Rick is obviously a twentieth-century person. So why does he like to write so much about the past? 'I used to hate history at school. I used to go into the cafe and play the pinball machines instead. I thought it was the most boring subject in the world. But I must admit history makes the present day and I am fascinated by our past. Basically, what we do today dictates what tomorrow is going to be like. You prepare for the future by comparing with the past, so there is really no such thing as present. I'm very fond of pageantry. I love English pageantry. And although I've been lucky enough to travel round the world, I realize how unlucky some countries are to have no heritage. I mean, you go to America and a guy says: "This is the oldest building in our town - it's thirty-six years old." They've got nothing. Nobody's got anything to compare with what we have in Britain.'

So that's Rick - past, present and future. I left him to sum up his career so far.

'It's very hard to analyse myself. I can't go into the audience and look at myself. I can't listen to a piece of my music for the first time like everyone else. I can't look at my career objectively . . . only the public can do that. Only they can judge whether everything I've been through to bring my music to the world has been worth it.

'All my life I have striven to create music I believed in wholeheartedly. In the course of doing that, and winning the respect of audiences, I wanted to sell lots of records and make a lot of money. The big aim was to make myself happy and secure by doing something I believed in. This will sound very egotistical, but when you succeed it's an incredible feeling, but you don't think: "Right, I've done it. I'll pack it in now." You get a great surge to work harder and create better music.'

Thus spake the Caped Crusader.

NINETEEN

Roundabout

Roundabout is an apt word to describe the astonishing change in the life style of Rick and *Yes* since he re-joined the group. For years he has been the rock world's most legendary drinker, while Jon, Chris and Steve rarely supped anything stronger than grape juice.

But now a near-fatal liver disease caused by too much drinking - two bottles of whisky a day, plus bottles of port, and pint after pint of beer - has forced the Caped Crusader to become a teetotaller.

There are no more of those wild, crazy, alcoholic binges for which Wakeman became so famous. And now while his *Yes* friends enjoy a quiet drink after a concert Rick sticks to Perrier Water or Seven Up.

'I've had to quit drinking for good,' explained Rick. 'My doctor told me that my liver had gone and I either had to stop drinking immediately or I'd be dead in a short time.

Having already suffered a heart attack, I had to take notice of what he said. If somebody gives you the choice of living or dying you choose life. I suppose you could say that I had become an alcoholic. Alcoholics don't; like to admit it, but I must have been one.'

Wakeman became seriously ill again in June, 1977, while in London to record the 'Tormato' album with *Yes*. By then he had already cut down considerably on his boozing, but previous excesses and late hours had caught up with him.

'I was permanently sick and incredibly tired for about two weeks. I was sleeping up to 15 hours a day and as soon as I got up I felt I had to go straight back to bed again. I kept falling asleep. Then blisters began coming up on my feet and I couldn't wear shoes for two weeks. It was really frightening.

'My problem was that I had had a huge capacity for drink. If I had been drunk after five double scotches like the average person, I would never have got on stage night after night. But I could drink bottles of scotch and port, and pints of beer, without them having any serious effect on me. I would then go on stage as if nothing had happened. Looking back I don't know how I got into such a state.

'Some people have the DT's. I had the DD's - too many Double Diamonds. I still go into pubs, but now

I only drink lemonade or mineral water. I've found that the best doctor in the world is your body. It tells you when something is wrong and then you've got to heed the warning signs.'

Wakeman told me of his new life without drink just before he began work on his latest epic solo album, 'The Seven Wonders of the World'.

He added: 'Considering the way I have abused my body with my drinking, I must be one of those seven wonders to still be alive.' But no longer being an imbiber has brought Rick one big worry and that is whether he will still be allowed to be Chairman of the 'Over the Top Club', a bizarre organization based in London, whose members are some of the more eccentric characters of the rock world.

'I am very worried about whether they will let me continue as President now that I have given up drink,' he told me. 'I believe that they have been holding emergency meetings long into the night to see whether I can remain a member.'

I talked to Allan James, one of the founders of this club, which had its wacky inauguration in a top London restaurant at Christmas, 1976. Then the clubbers were so wild in their antics that they were promptly asked to leave and banned for life by the management. Since then two other restaurants have closed their doors to this group of raucous rockers, which include disc jockeys Alan Freeman, Kid Jensen and Peter Powell, and two former members of Deep Purple, Jon Lord and David Coverdale, both now with *Whitesnake*.

'The club is a mixture of guys in the music business who get together as an excuse to get drunk,' explained Allan James, who does radio and television promotion for *Yes*. 'Women aren't allowed.'

'Our meetings are absolutely hilarious. Like the one we had in one of London's poshest restaurants. We booked the place and then told members that they had to come in strange attire. I dressed up as Mother Christmas, all in red, and two others came in equally strange outfits. One wore a lady's nightdress. We all just walked in this staid place and sat down at our tables and promptly began pouring wine over each other and hurling food. Of course we didn't throw it at anyone else in the restaurant! All our meetings take the same pattern.

'Rick became involved in the club at my 30th birthday party. He went over the top so quickly that we just had to make him chairman. He walked in after flying from Switzerland and proposed a toast to me. "Gentlemen, I give you Jamesey," he said. Then he promptly began pouring wine all over me. Everyone else joined in and I was covered from head to foot. Then he picked up my lovely birthday cake and pushed it right in my face. Then food started coming at me from all angles. When Alan Freeman turned up he poured a bottle of wine over him, then picked up a bottle and poured it over another disc jockey who wasn't doing any harm to anybody. It was a birthday party that I'll never forget.'

The big question I had to put to Mr James was, could an abstaining Wakeman still hold onto his office in the club? 'Of course he can,' he said. 'But now, instead of wine, he'll have orange juice thrown over him instead.'

No doubt those outraged diners think it's criminal what Rick and his cronies get up to. Wakeman won't agree. But he has a strange fascination with crime and criminals. And that brought the inspiration for his eighth solo album, 'Rick Wakeman's Criminal Record'.

Rick had met train robber Ronnie Biggs in Brazil and had also corresponded with the infamous Kray

Twins in Parkhurst Prison, where they are serving 30 years for murder - they have many of his albums in their cells.

While *Yes* were recording 'Going for the One', Rick was talking to some roadies about this subject. One of them jokingly asked, 'What's your criminal record, Rick?' That comment struck a chord in the maestro's mind. 'That's just the theme I need for my next album,' he said. The disc, not one of Rick's biggest sellers but still technically brilliant, was recorded in Montreux, immediately after the *Yes* album was completed. Wakeman produced the album himself, with John Timperley and Dave Richards engineering.

He said that he wanted it to cover as many facets of crime as he could without naming specific deeds. The track titles supply sufficient hints to fire the imagination: 'Statue of Justice' - named after the figure on top of the Old Bailey - 'Crime of Passion', 'Chamber of Horrors' and so on.

'Statue of Justice' owes much to Chris Squire who left the tape running after a 'Going for the One' session in which Rick was playing piano. While the others went for a break, Rick continued to improvise for about 20 minutes. When Chris told him that he had been taped. Rick asked to hear it back and later used part of the recording on that track.

While the overall theme of the album is crime, the execution is lightly impressionistic rather than sombre, blending rock and classical elements effortlessly, on a grand and sweeping scale. On the 'Birdman of Alcatraz' Rick used twelve pianos and an aviary of tropical birds. It's Wakeman at his most serious - none of the synthesised satire that brings a certain sly light-heartedness to several of the other cuts. 'The Breathalyzer', a possibly autobiographical, blues-orientated number about a drunk being busted, includes a 20-second vocal by Bill Oddie, of 'Goodies' fame. Its intent and purpose, as quickly becomes apparent, is sheer, outrageous fun. In 'Judas Iscariot', Wakeman opens in Bach-like style - this track was recorded on a church organ in Vevey, Switzerland - and builds grandly, with a barrage of synthesizers and a large angelic chorus, to an overwhelming finale.

While in London in October, 1978, for the four *Yes* Wembley shows which attracted some 80,000 fans to the Empire Pool, Rick met up with another extraordinary criminal - Maurice O'Mahoney, nicknamed King Squealer. A villain from the age of ten, he turned Queen's evidence, informing on more than 200 crooks who had been involved in crimes totalling more than two million pounds. Now a £20,000 underworld 'contract' is out for his life.

Rick had agreed to write the foreword to O'Mahoney's book 'King Squealer' (W. H. Allen). So the ex-gangster wanted to thank Rick personally for his endorsement of the book. He did some detective work of his own and found Rick had checked into a London hotel under a false name (as usual). This time, O'Mahoney discovered it was as 'Hugh Rinal.' (Sometimes he uses 'Ivor Biggun.')

Rick was so pleased to meet him that he became an honoured guest for the shows and Rick let him travel around as a VIP in his Rolls-Royce. 'It's a pity I didn't meet you before I recorded 'Criminal Record',' he told the Mo, 'I could have done a track about you.'

The bizarre title of *Yes*'s album 'Tormato' was the product of a photo-session in Devon at a place called Yes Tor and an incident in which Steve Howe threw a tomato at the proposed sleeve picture. After seeing the splattered result they thought up the play-on-words title.

The album coincided with the band's tenth anniversary and followed another record-breaking tour of

America. At Madison Square Garden they played four sell-out concerts, clocking up another 80,000 customers and earning them the coveted Golden Ticket Award for £1 million box office takings.

Since Rick rejoined they have consolidated their position as one of the biggest grossing rock acts in the world.

A highlight of the shows was the £50,000 revolving stage, which turns completely once every four minutes and allows every fan to see all the band. Another welcome sight for the audiences was Rick in his cape again. At Wembley he wore a space-man-style gold caped suit with RCW – Richard Christopher Wakeman - inscribed on it. He had decided to replace the famous glittering capes with jumpsuits during the 'Going for the One' tour after nearly strangling himself.

'The problem was his keyboards were then at two levels, and he nearly got hung on one occasion during rehearsals when the cape got caught between the two keyboards],' explained John Bollenberg, President of Rick's fan club in Europe - the official Rick Wakeman Information Centre based at Zwaluwenstraat 114B, Bus l, 8400 Ostend, Belgium.

'So he had to find another way of dressing for the tour. He quickly got in touch with the designer of Elvis Presley's clothes and ordered two jumpsuits from him. One was white and the other was blue and covered with birds and stars. But now he's back with his keyboards on one level and so has reverted to his capes.'

During 1978, Rick was paid the biggest tribute so far in his career, when the Royal Philharmonic Orchestra of England released an album on A & M called 'The Royal Philharmonic Orchestra Performs the best known works of Rick Wakeman'. Rick was chosen as 'a composer whose work was of the quality and

the style to make transcription into a purely symphonic format warranted and interesting.'

The album, which includes excerpts from 'The Myths and Legends of King Arthur and the Knights of the Round Table', 'The Six Wives of Henry VIII', 'Journey to the Centre of the Earth', and 'White Rock', was arranged and conducted by Yorkshire-born Richard Hartley, who has also composed the soundtrack scores for 'The Romantic Englishman' and 'Aces High.'

Robin Geoffrey Cable, who is a well-known producer of many internationally recognised musicians, including Harry Nilsson, Queen and Jimmy Webb, explained how the album was recorded:-

'The conventional technique of recording a symphony orchestra is to use one central stereo microphone to record the whole orchestra, backed up by a few others for emphasis on particular sections of it. However, this doesn't give the same degree of control possible in the recording of a rock band. So for this album we decided to record the orchestra in sections and give each instrument an individual microphone. This made the recording a far more complex procedure but we used the NECAM computer-assisted mixing system which enabled us to have complete control over the position and presence of each instrument at all times.

'Using these techniques did create a number of problems. A rock band has a strong rhythm section, which is usually the first element of the music to be recorded and forms the basis over which the other instruments can be over-dubbed, but this isn't true of a symphony orchestra. The solution we found was to synchronise the sections of the orchestra using n system of pulse beats which the musicians heard over their headphones.

'The second major problem was that a symphony orchestra recorded in sections in a studio does not have the same ambience that it would have in a concert hall. But we were able to simulate the same aural environment at the mixing stage by using four stereo EMT l40 and 240 reverberation units and a special tape delay effect.'

Through their expertise Hartley and Cable produced a superb showcase for Rick Wakeman's genius.

The album is further recognition of Wakeman's status as a composer, a 'serious' musician whose work will survive him. But Rick is still finding new ideas, reaching the end of previously untrodden musical paths before others have even started the journey.

Each album is exciting and original. Where will the Wakeman roundabout take him next?

FACING PAGE: Rick Wakeman and Dan Wooding at the BBC

APPENDIX

RICK WAKEMAN'S KEYBOARDS

(As they were in 1978)

A Series 3C Moog Synthesizer
A Polymoog
Taunus Moog pedals
4 Birontrons
Steinway 9-foot Concert Grand Piano (standard condition).
Yamaha C3 Concert Grand Piano
Baldwin Electric Harpsichord (standard condition).
Godwin Organ Model SC 444 P (standard condition).
Fender Rhodes 88 Electric Piano (with built-in Phaser and Flanger customized by Systech).
Hohner Clavinette (with built-in Phaser by Systech).
RMI Rocksichord (with built-in Phaser by Toby Errington).
RMI Computer Piano (with built-in Echo by Echoplex).
6 Mini Moogs through a Digital Delay System.
2 Hammond C3 Organs. This has a special switch box, which enables the sound to go through a standard cabinet or two Leslies with phasers built by Systech. It also has extra percussion tabs.
Pedals: volume pedals only by Systech.
Amps: 2 x 400 W. Phase Linear Amps.
Speakers: 2 J.B.L. 18-inch with 4 J.B.L. horns specially designed to low frequency to contain the Moogs.
Effects: Roland Space Echo and a Echoplex echo unit, Lexicon digital delay, phasers, flngers by Systech.
A Helpinstill grand-piano pick-up is used for 'live' work.

All of these are controlled by Toby Errington in a Soundcraft 6-in, 2-out Mixing Desk. The Harpsichord and the Godwin organ are put through Vortex and Sisco Rotary Cabinets.

The Monitor Cabinets contain 2 18-inch J.B.L. speakers and lens horns. Rick also owns a portable church/pipe organ, specially built for him by Noel Mander & Sons in London, and believed to be the only one of its type in the world.

RICK'S ALBUMS

(1970-77)

With Strawbs:

'Dragonfly', played as session musician (A&M , AMLS 970) 1970.
'Just a Collection of Antiques and Curi0s' (A&M , AMLS 994) 1970.
'From the Witchwood' (A&M , AMLH 64304) 1971.
With Yes:

'Fragile' (Atlantic, K50009) 1971.
'Close to the Edge' (Atlantic, KSOOIQ) 1972.
'Yessongs' (Atlantic, K60045) 1973.
'Tales from Topographic Oceans' (Atlantic, K80001) 1973.
'Going for the One' (Atlantic K50379) 1977
Solo:

'Piano Vibrations' (Polydor, 2460 135) 1971.
'The Six Wives of Henry VIII' (A&M , AMLH 64361) 1973.
'Journey to the Centre of the Earth' (A&M , AMLH 63621) 1974.
'The Myths and Legends of King Arthur and the Knights of the Round Table' (A&M , AMLH 64515) 1975.
'Lisztomania' (A&M , AMLH 64546) 1975.
'No Earthly Connection' (A&M , AMLH 64583) 1976.
'White Rock' (A&M , AMLH 64614) 1977.
'Rick Wakeman's Criminal Record' (A&M , AMLH 64660) 1977.

FILMS

Zee & Co. (part of soundtrack).
Lisztomania (co-composed and arranged, and recorded score).
White Rock (composed and recorded score).

I would like to thank:– Rosaline Wakeman, Mr. & Mrs. C. Wakeman and complete family tree, Mrs. Symes, Mr. Herrera, the Atlantic Blues, the Concord Quartet, the Royal College of Music, The Strawbs and Roadies, David Katz, The Ronnie Smith Band, James Royal, A & M Records, The Music Press, Dan Wooding, David Bowie, Brian Lane, Lew Warbourton, Stanley Myers and all Session Mo's Tony Brainsby, Keith Goodwin, The Yes and Roadies, Annakata Music, Paramount, Screen Gems, All the London Recording Studios and Engineers, Essex Music, Toni Visconti, Gus Dudgeon, Jon Anthony, Eddie Offord, The Musical Bargain Centre, The Tony Oee Showband, Dan Wooding, South Harrow Baptist Church, Wolfgang Amadeus Motzart, Arnolo, Martin and Morrow, Sid Sax, Charlie Katz, All session Musicians, The White Bear Hounslow, The BBC, Colin Spiers, Roy Shea, Ex-members and Performers of Booze-Proof (White Hart Acton), Becky Appold, Jon Schroeder, God Bless Brentford Football Club, Ken Scott, Piglet, the Top Rank Reading, The Woolfords, The Spinning Wheel, Roger Dean, Staff and Pupils of Drayton Manor County Grammar School and all my friends off and on the road too numerous to mention for helping to further my career either deliberately or by accident. P.S. One future offspring. Love to Everybody.